Talking to My Father

What Jesus Teaches About Prayer

RAY C. STEDMAN

MULTNOMAH PRESS
PORTLAND, OREGON 97266

Unless otherwise identified, all Scripture references are from the Revised Standard Version of the Bible, copyright 1946, 1952, © 1971, 1973, Division of Christian Education, National Council of the Churches of Christ in the USA. Used by permission.

Cover design by Phil Malyon and Judy Quinn
Photograph by Robert Cushman Hayes

TALKING TO MY FATHER
© 1975 by Ray C. Stedman
Published by Multnomah Press
Portland, Oregon 97266

Printed in the United States of America

Library of Congress Cataloging in Publication Data

Stedman, Ray C.
    Talking to my Father.

    Reprint. Originally published: Jesus teaches on prayer.
Waco, Tex. : Word Books, c1975. (Discovery books)
    1. Jesus Christ—Prayers.   I. Title.
BV229.S74   1984   248.3'2   84-20783
ISBN 0-88070-075-0

84 85 86 87 88 89 90 − 10 9 8 7 6 5 4 3 2 1

CONTENTS

PART I

We must either be praying or fainting—there is no other alternative. The purpose of all faith is to bring us into direct, personal, vital touch with God. True prayer is an awareness of our helpless need and an acknowledgement of divine adequacy. For Jesus, prayer was as necessary as breathing, the very breath of his life. Although God certainly knows all our needs, praying for them changes our attitudes from complaint to praise and enables us to participate in God's personal plans for our lives.

And he told them a parable, to the effect that they ought always to pray and not lose heart. He said, "In a certain city there was a judge who neither feared God nor regarded man; and there was a widow in that city who kept coming to him and saying, 'Vindicate me against my adversary.' For a while he refused; but afterward he said to himself, 'Though I neither fear God nor regard man, yet because this widow bothers me, I will vindicate her, or she will wear me out by her continual coming.'" And the Lord said, "Hear what the unrighteous judge says. And will not God vindicate his elect, who cry to him day and night? Will he delay long over them? I tell you, he will vindicate them speedily. Nevertheless, when the Son of man comes, will he find faith on earth?" (Luke 18:1-8).

1
WHY PRAY?

All of us are familiar with the vivid way metaphor and simile can set truth before us. We are continually using such figures, likening and contrasting one thing to another.

Sometimes comparison can be very vivid: "As nervous as a long-tailed cat in a room full of rocking chairs," or "as helpless as a trombone player in a telephone booth." But contrast is an equally effective way to emphasize truth and make it vivid, and this is the form our Lord employs in this teaching on prayer.

When I was in college I had a roommate who was six feet, seven inches tall, and he weighed two hundred and sixty-five pounds. His nickname, of

course, was "Tiny." And what poor fellow, possessor
of a shiny, hairless pate, has not been called "Curly"
at one time or another? This common form of contrast calls constant attention to an outstanding characteristic.

An Inescapable Choice

It is significant that this word on prayer from the
lips of Jesus immediately follows the account of his
second coming, the parallel passage in Luke to the
Olivet Discourse in the Gospel of Matthew. Our Lord
moves immediately from his word concerning his
coming to this word about prayer, indicating the direct correlation between watchfulness and prayer.

Our Lord brings the subject of prayer into sharp
focus through the use of three deliberate contrasts.
There is, first, a contrast of principles. Luke is careful
to indicate the point Jesus intended to make. He
says, "he told them a parable to the effect that they
ought always to pray and not lose heart," or, as the
King James has it, "not faint." By this Jesus means
most simply that we are to pray and not quit. It is an
exhortation to persistence in prayer. But it also implies a contrast. Here Jesus boldly confronts us with
an inescapable choice: We must either pray or faint,
one or the other. Either we learn to cry out to an unseen Father who is ever present with us, or else we
will lose heart; there are no other alternatives.

Some may challenge that. What about these
people, they ask, who seem to find much "joie de
vivre" (joy of life) without being Christians? They
seldom or never pray. Have they not discovered a way
of life that can be meaningful and exciting without
recourse to prayer or to religious faith? This question
is worthy of at least some brief examination. Who has

not seen such people and wondered if perhaps they have found another alternative, another answer?

Yet when we observe carefully these who seem to have found the secrets of life, who appear to live in an exciting world of adventure and romance, we are frequently surprised by obvious signs of despair, unsuspected by the general public—sudden manifestations of fainting. Think, for example, of men like Ernest Hemingway, Jack London, and other literary idols who appeared for many years to have found the secret of intense living but who ultimately demonstrated that all along there had been an inner fainting, an inner losing of heart.

Is there anything more pathetic today than the tortured groping of millions of people frantically trying to find life? And this condition is found not only among the aged, who have had their fling at life and feel they have nothing left, but just as frequently among young people whose life seems to stretch out before them, waiting to be lived.

Not long ago I had three young men in my study, all of them under twenty years of age, and each in his own way expressed to me his view of life. In words sometimes faltering, sometimes eloquent, each one said that he found life dull and without challenge. All three were looking for a light to follow, a cause to live for. Having not even reached the age of twenty, life ahead of them looked dull and uninviting.

A Hollow God

Why? Surely this is the harvest of a very widespread philosophy today. It is the idea that we live in an impersonal universe—a great, remorseless machine, obeying relentless laws in the midst of which we tiny humans are nothing but transient pygmies. Where did this idea originate? It comes from our enthusiastic enthronement of an agnostic science as god.

Of course, we all owe a great deal to true science. Our vaunted comforts and luxuries—even our necessities—come to us through this avenue. But science is in grave danger of being exalted in the eyes of many as a kind of god. We have built an altar to science, and burned incense before it.

But the trouble with this god is that it is hollow; it is a god which has no heart, no compassion. Science cannot feel or laugh or show mercy. It can only analyze and measure; dissect, speculate, and weigh. The universe as seen through the eyes of such a god is likewise impersonal, cold, relentless, distant.

The result is that we have in our day, more than at any other time in human history, a generation that has been raised without a Heavenly Father. The agony that we hear is nothing but the cry of orphaned lostness. This is why the great thinkers who write from this point of view inevitably end up as pessimists. They give expression to what has been so eloquently termed, "the tragic sense of life." Read it in Bertrand Russell and other leaders of modern thought. Our continual mad carousel of amusement and pleasure is only an anesthetic to dull the ache of an empty heart. Jesus was right when he said there are only two alternatives: Either we pray or we faint.

Beyond the things which science can measure and weigh and analyze, beyond this cold, impersonal universe, Jesus says, is a Father's heart. Around us are a Father's arms, and we are to cry out to him, for in Christ his voice has already called to us. We are to answer like a child crying out to his father. For, like a child, we do not always know what is wrong with us.

Helmut Thielicke suggests that sometimes a child can only look at his mother with great, appealing eyes and cannot say what is wrong; but his mother usually knows, for she takes hold at the right places. "As a father pities his children [the Scripture says], so the Lord pities those who fear him" (Psalm 103:13). We may cry out to him when we are in trouble and even though we may cry out about the wrong thing, nevertheless, when we cry out, a Father hears and a Father's strength moves to act on our behalf. In this contrast of principles, then, we have the whole point of the story Jesus tells.

Now in the story itself, there is also a contrast of persons. It is really twofold—first, the widow and the judge. Who is more proverbially weak and defenseless than a widow? A writer who wants to portray some scheming rascal out to deprive someone of their livelihood usually depicts his victim as a widow. Then, in contrast, there is the judge. Who can be more hardboiled and unyielding than a judge, especially an unrighteous judge? Here is a tough, hard-bitten, self-centered old skinflint, with a heart as cold as a bathroom floor at two o'clock in the morning!

See how harsh he is! The widow had a persecutor, someone who was harassing her, and she appealed for help. But the judge couldn't care less; he was utterly unmoved by her pleas and nothing could reach him. Since he was a godless judge, there was no moving of his affections with the lever of morality. And he had no regard for persons, so no political pressure could influence him. In view of the judge's hardness of heart the case for the widow is absolutely hopeless. Nothing she can do will move this man to intercede in her case.

The Widow's Key

Nevertheless, Jesus said, she found a way by proceeding to make life utterly miserable for him. She gave him no rest day and night. She was continually before his court, hounding him, harassing him, plaguing him, until finally the judge was forced to act. To get rid of her he granted her request, and she got what she needed!

Right here lies the whole point of the story. What is Jesus after? He is indicating that this widow found the secret of handling reluctant judges! She discovered, in other words, the key to power. She found the one principle on which even a reluctant judge would act, despite his formidable defenses. That principle was persistence.

Now, says Jesus, prayer is the corresponding principle which is the key to the Fatherheart of God. Persistent pressure was the key to this unrighteous judge; perpetual prayer is the key to the activity of God.

When, like the widow, life appears to us to be hopeless and useless, when we are victims of forces which are greater than we can manage (and who of us has not felt life to be this?), when no openings appear in the wall of pressure which rings us about, when there is no answer to the inescapable problems before us and there is no end in sight but certain failure or loss, Jesus says there is still one way out. There is a way to the place of power; there is a way to a certain solution of our problems, an answer to the unbearable pressure. It is the answer of prayer; of crying out to a God we cannot see but whom we may rely upon, a Father with a father's heart and a father's tender compassion and willingness to act. Prayer, he says, *always* stirs the heart of God, *always* moves God to act.

No Pickets Needed

But there is yet another contrast of persons intended here, for Jesus particularly says that God is *not* like the unrighteous judge, that he *will not* delay an answer to our prayers, that he does *not* require continual battering to get him to move.

> *Hear what the unrighteous judge says. And will not God vindicate his elect, who cry to him day and night? Will he delay long over them? I tell you, he will vindicate them speedily (Luke 18:6-8a).*

It is sometimes taught that Jesus is here encouraging what is called "prevailing prayer," which is often another way of describing an attempt to belabor God, to give him no peace, to picket the throne of heaven until we get the request we want. But this is an unbiblical and unchristian attitude in prayer, though it is frequently held.

Some years ago an article appeared in the newspaper about a man in Missouri who announced that he was troubled about world conditions, particularly about the moral conditions of this country, and had determined to fast and pray until God sent a great awakening to correct the moral degeneracy of the day. He announced that he would keep on even until death, if necessary, asking God to move.

The papers carried the story of his fast day after day. His strength began to fail, he grew weaker and weaker, and finally was confined to his bed. Bulletins were issued each day following his condition. He was evidently a man of unusual determination—most of us would have quit after the third day and settled for a good beefsteak, but this man did not. He went on with his fast until he actually died. The funeral was widely covered and many lauded his remarkable persistence.

But was that really prayer? No, it was not! It was an attempt to blackmail God. This man was holding his own life as a pistol to the head of God and demanding all his money! He was insisting that God

move on his terms and according to his time
schedule. That is not prayer.

Lost in the Woods

Jesus says that God is not an unrighteous God like
the old judge in the story, demanding that we
wheedle and struggle and persuade him to move. He
is not grudging. No, prayer is the cry of a beloved
child to his father, and frequently it is the cry of a
child who is lost in dark woods, with noises in the
brush—strange, frightening noises. The child may
cry out to be led to an open road, or to be home safe in
bed, or at least to see a light in the distance so he can
know his way. But such prayer is not always answered
that way, for God is a Father and, as Jesus said in
another place, he knows already what we have need of
before we pray.

Paul reminds us in Romans 12 that often we do not
know what to pray for, but God knows. The Father
knows because he is a father, and he also knows when
to answer in the particular way we have asked and
when it may not be the best thing to do, or even the
possible thing, under the circumstances.

Yes, it is true; *that* answer may indeed be long delayed, but there is no delay at all in *an* answer to our
prayer. What Jesus is saying is that when we cry out
there is *immediately* an answer, *without* delay—*speedily*
God rushes to the help, to the succor, of his child.

The answer may be the squeeze of a Father's hand
on ours, the quiet comfort of a Father's voice, the
reassurance of a Father's presence even though the
woods are still dark and the noises are growing
louder. There is an immediate answering assurance
that the Father is with us and in his own time and way
will lead us to the house and put us safely in bed, or
bring us to light again. Surely this is what Jesus

means, "And will not God vindicate his elect, who cry to him day and night? Will he delay long over them? I tell you, he will vindicate them speedily" (vv. 7, 8).

Which Do You Prefer?

Jesus ends his story abruptly with a third contrast, the contrast of practice: "Nevertheless, when the Son of man comes, will he find faith on earth?" (v. 8). Notice Jesus does not say, "When the Son of man comes, he will *not* find faith on earth," nor does he say, "When the Son of man comes, he *will* find faith on earth." He leaves it as a question, hanging in the air, uncertain, unanswered.

But there is no doubt at all about the faithfulness of the Son of man. He will come. The uncertainty is entirely in the latter part of the sentence. He does not say, "If the Son of man comes," but "When"; for this is one thing that is absolutely certain. It does not rest upon man, his faithfulness or his faithlessness; it rests only upon the sovereign determination of God. There is not the slightest doubt but that God is ready to do exactly what he says he will do in any circumstance at any time. There is with him no shadow of turning; he is not a respecter of persons; there are no divisions or discriminations among men with him. God is utterly faithful; it is man who raises the doubts.

But we do not often see it that way. To us, it is God that fails. After all, what is behind the frenzied clamor after the gifts of the Holy Spirit today? Meetings are held to pray for power, or for tongues, or for revival. Might this not really be a subtle attempt to blackmail God, or at least to blame him for our weaknesses? Are we not saying, "Lord, the trouble is that you have not given us all we need. You have not made everything available to us. You are holding back, you are reluctant; you give only grudgingly and often won't give us what we lack. If we only had *this*, then we could work for you."

But Jesus is saying, no, that is not true. It is not fair to put the blame on him, for God is utterly faithful. There has never been anything lacking from his side. But, he implies, is it not possible that men *prefer* weakness to power? Do they not prefer anxiety to peace, frenzy to rest, doubt to confidence, fear to faith, or malice to love? Is it not possible that because of this human tendency, when the Son of man comes he will not find faith on the earth? If there is an apparent failure in prayer, it is not God's fault but man's.

Notice something else; he does not ask, "When the Son of man comes, will he find men praying?" He has been speaking of prayer but now his question is, "When the Son of man comes, will he find faith?" Doubtless the reason for this change is that prayer is faith expressed. True prayer is not begging or cajoling a reluctant God. That is never prayer! True prayer is believing, it is faith. Prayer is thanking instead of complaining, trusting instead of trying, rejoicing, accepting, appropriating, receiving—that is prayer.

A Matter of Relationship

Well, someone may say, if there is a Father out there, and he is so eager to give to us and knows what we need—and especially since we're so apt to pray the wrong prayer anyway—why bother to pray?

The answer to this frequently raised question is that the purpose of prayer is clearly to bring us into an understanding of the Father's heart: It brings us, not always to the place of an answer, but to the place where a direct answer is unnecessary, to an understanding of the program and the purpose of the Father.

After all, relationship with God cannot exist without communication. Everyone knows of couples that have stopped speaking to each other. Such a marriage is a disintegrating union, a dead relationship. Human desires and needs require speech; they must be expressed; there must be interchange, a flow of words for a marriage to be a live, fruitful, vital relationship. Prayer also is an absolute necessity in the interchange of a child's heart with the Father.

This is why Jesus asked: When he comes, will he find men exercising this blessed privilege? Will he find them expressing themselves, pouring out everything without halt or hindrance to the Father? Uttering the resentments as well as the joys, the complaints, the feelings of the heart in its deepest moods—will he find men like that? That is the true expression of faith. To fail to pray *that* way is inevitably to stop talking with God, to lose communication altogether.

One sign of losing communication is when we become obsessed with talk about God. When men only talk about God instead of with God they are manifesting a deteriorated faith, for the purpose of all faith is to bring us into direct, personal, vital touch with God. The mark of a decadent religion is invariably that men are deeply engrossed in discussions *about* God, spending hours in lengthy, theological debate about the nature and character of God. But as Luther very aptly put it, "You that manifest a concern about religion, why don't you pray?"

> *Our Father, these words of our Lord Jesus have made us aware of the lack of faith in our lives. We cry out to you now in our weakness and our failure to exercise faith and say, O Father, teach us to pray. Teach us to be men and women who depend*

*continually upon you, who are pouring out to you
every aspect of our life without hindrance, without
reservation, telling you all things, and listening to
you about all things. In Jesus' name, Amen.*

He also told this parable to some who trusted in them-selves that they were righteous and despised others: "Two men went up into the temple to pray, one a Pharisee and the other a tax collector. The Pharisee stood and prayed thus with himself, 'God, I thank thee that I am not like other men, extortioners, unjust, adulterers, or even like this tax collector. I fast twice a week, I give tithes of all that I get.' But the tax collector, standing far off, would not even lift up his eyes to heaven, but beat his breast, saying, 'God, be merciful to me a sinner!' I tell you, this man went down to his house justified rather than the other; for every one who exalts himself will be humbled, but he who humbles himself will be exalted" (Luke 18:9-14).

2
THE NATURE
OF PRAYER

In this parable about prayer, our Lord minces no words about the need of prayer: *Men must either pray or faint.* If we are fainting, then no matter how much we may think otherwise, we are not really praying. If we are truly praying, we are not fainting. The Lord puts it on an either-or basis.

But like this Pharisee, you may say, "I *am* praying. I pray thirty minutes every morning and ten minutes every night, and I am even one of those few who faithfully meet with a mid-week prayer group, but still there is much fainting in my experience, life is not satisfying to me—I am not really living." Or perhaps you are among those who must admit in all honesty that there is very little prayer in your life. For many of us it is hard to pray and easy to find something else to do.

Not More Prayer

But even if you resolve to try harder to put more prayer into your life, it will not be long before you will become aware, as perhaps you already are, that this is not the answer: It will really change nothing. Scheduling more time for prayer is not necessarily the solution.

Is it possible that our Lord is wrong then when he says, either pray or faint? Is it really *that* much of an issue? Could it be that we *are* praying, and yet we faint? If it seems so, perhaps we need to discover more about the nature of prayer. It may be that we need a new kind of prayer, not just more of the same kind.

True prayer is not a difficult thing. It is natural, instinctive, and comes easily. This *kind* of prayer is the key to God's power and glory. True prayer is an open channel to the *eagerness of God to help us.* To help us in this, Jesus moves right on from a discussion of the need of prayer to the parable of the Pharisee and the tax collector, where he teaches the nature of authentic prayer. These two parables must be taken together.

We could call this story, "The Parable of the Two Prayers," for it begins with the words, "Two men went up into the temple to pray." The object of our Lord in telling this parable is not to illustrate what self-righteousness is (though that is certainly involved), but he is still on the subject of prayer, and here he tells us what real prayer is. Furthermore, the structure of this parable, like the other, is one of contrast. Our Lord is teaching truth by setting it alongside error; as we see the error we can, by contrast, understand and grasp the truth.

The Pharisee was a man of prayer: He prayed frequently and punctiliously. But though he was faithful in prayer, his prayer was entirely wrong. The tax collector, or publican, on the other hand, is not accustomed to praying; he is infrequently found in the temple courts. This is all new to him, but his prayer is exactly right. As we examine these two portrayals of prayer, let's see if we can grasp the lessons Jesus wants us to learn.

In observing the Pharisee we learn what prayer is *not;* here is a form of praying which is not prayer. At the outset it *looks* good. He stood, Jesus said, with his arms spread and his eyes lifted up to heaven. Among the Jews, this was the prescribed posture for prayer. But, says Jesus, he prayed thus *"with himself."* What a keen thrust that is! He was not praying to God; he was praying to himself. There was no one at the other end of the line! This prayer was a total waste of time. He may have been doing what some modern writers say is the true nature of prayer—"communing with the inner man"—but he certainly was not reaching any higher. He was not touching God; our Lord makes that point clear.

Who's a Pharisee?

What more can we learn from this man about how *not* to pray? Well, it is clear that it is not prayer to approach God *impressed with our own virtues.* This man stood and prayed, "God, I thank thee that I am not like other men, extortioners, unjust, adulterers, or even like this tax collector." He was obviously well impressed with what he felt were his claims upon God's attention. This man felt that God ought to be thanked for having made such a remarkable specimen of humanity, and if no one else would do it, he would take on the task himself.

We laugh as we listen to his prayer, but don't we often unconsciously reflect the same position? We often pray like this, "Lord, come and help me to do this task." We mean by this, "I will contribute my ability to exercise leadership, my talents for singing or speaking, and then, Lord, will you pour on the magic powder of Spirit-power? Then you and I together will enjoy great success." In other words, we follow the philosophy in praying, "I'll do my best and God can do the rest."

It isn't that we exclude him and say, "I can do it all," but we say, "Lord, I have a part that I can contribute which you desperately need, and I am willing to invest my ability in this enterprise if you will do the rest. You must do something, but I must do something too." I suspect that most Christian prayers are prayed from this position.

Sometimes the virtue we contribute to the program of God is "humility." There is a kind of reverse brand of Pharisaism among Christians which goes something like this: "Thank God, I am not as proud as this Pharisee is." We make ourselves out to be utterly vile, babbling continually about our shortcomings and our sins. We say, "Lord, I *am* an extortioner, I *am* unjust, I *am* an adulterer; I commit fornication twice a week, I admit it. I don't kid myself, I'm honest enough to admit that I am a louse." And thereby we hope to impress God with our honesty and our humility.

But the simple truth is that we have no virtues of our own to contribute, none whatsoever. We have absolutely nothing to add to God's cause. We are praying out of utter bankruptcy, and if we are honest we will admit it. We forget that the very talents with which we identify ourselves, the abilities that we have for leadership or speaking or singing are in themselves gifts of God. They do not belong to us but are simply on loan. They already belong to God.

Isn't it strange how easily we identify ourselves with our virtues and disclaim identity with our faults? Our failures we blame on everyone else; for our successes we take full credit. But there is so much we forget. We forget God's shielding grace that has saved us from some of the terrible things others have fallen into, and for which we look down our noses at them. We forget that possibly the only reason we are not standing in that poor wretch's shoes (who has been guilty of such vile and repulsive things) is simply that we have never been exposed to them. Are we sure we would not have fallen, too, had we been there? And we forget some of the things that are actually present in our lives—we forget our clever manipulations, our deliberate deceits, our phony sympathies, our dubious business arrangements. We are careful to remember only our virtues.

How do we become so impressed with ourselves? Like this Pharisee, we look downward. As he looked down on this tax collector, he immediately felt virtuous. "Lord, I thank you that I am not like that. *I* don't do any of those things." He had taken a vantage point on the scale of human morals which permitted him to look down. It is easy to do. There are always people who are worse than we are, and what a comfort they are to our hearts! This is why we love to gossip. What else explains the peculiar delight we take in sinking our teeth into someone else's reputation?

It is usually because it makes us feel superior. We delight in running someone else down because it makes us feel more virtuous. This is the point Jesus is making in describing the Pharisee. He says when we pray from this basis, when we approach God on this level, *we are praying with ourselves.* There is no real prayer. Our pious words, our properly phrased sentences, our completely orthodox approach is of no value whatever. We are praying out of an obsession with our own virtues.

Furthermore, Jesus says it is *not* prayer when we ask God's help because of our own accomplishments. This Pharisee said he fasted twice a week. That was much more than was required by the law which only commanded a fast once a year. He gave tithes of all he got, and that again was more than the law required. But he expected God to act on his behalf, because he felt God could hardly do otherwise in view of the fine record of faithful service he was able to lay before him. And do we not continually pray as though God owes us something?

> *"Lord, I have been faithfully teaching this Sunday school class for ten years. Surely now, Lord, you can do something for me."*

> *"Lord, I have been trying to be a good Christian parent and have done my best; now please keep my children from going astray during these difficult teen years."*

> *"Lord, I have given up so much for you, now give me this one little thing that I ask of you."*

Obviously there's a bit of Pharisee in each of us, isn't there?

But, someone says, Doesn't it say in Hebrews that God is not unrighteous to forget our labor of love (Hebrews 6:10)? Yes, it does, but if we approach God on that basis we have misunderstood the nature of prayer and missed the key to God's power.

It's Not Fair!

How revealing is that story of the old missionary couple who had been working in Africa for years and were returning from Africa to New York City to retire. They had no pension, for they belonged to no missionary board. Their health was broken; they were defeated, discouraged, and afraid. When they went down to the wharf to board the ship, they discovered they were booked on the same ship as President Teddy Roosevelt, who was returning from one of his big game hunting expeditions.

When they boarded the ship, no one paid any attention to them. They watched the tremendous fanfare that accompanied the President's arrival, with the band playing and passengers stationing themselves at vantage points to catch a glimpse of the great man.

As the ship moved across the ocean, the old missionary said to his wife, "Dear, something is wrong. Why should we have given our lives in faithful service for God in Africa all these many years and have no one care a thing about us? Here this man comes back from a big game hunting expedition and everybody makes much over him, but nobody gives two hoots about us."

His wife replied, "Dear, you shouldn't feel that way. Try not to be bitter about it." But he said, "I just can't help it; it doesn't seem right. After all, if God is running this world, why does he permit such injustice?"

As the boat neared the American shore, he became more and more depressed. And when the ship docked, a band was waiting to greet the President. The mayor of New York City was there, along with other leaders of the nation. The papers were full of the

President's arrival, but no one even noticed this missionary couple. They slipped off the ship and found a
cheap flat on the East side, hoping the next day to see
what they could do to make a living in the city.

But that night the man's spirit just broke. He said
to his wife, "I can't take this; God is not treating us
fairly. We don't even know anyone to help us, or
where to go. If God is a faithful God, why doesn't he
meet our need and send someone along?" His wife replied, "Why don't you go in the bedroom and talk to
the Lord about the whole thing?"

A short time later he came out from the bedroom,
but now his face was completely different. His wife
asked, "Dear, what happened? Everything is different, I can see. You feel better, don't you?" "Yes," he
said, "the Lord settled it with me. I went in and knelt
beside the bed and poured out the whole thing to
him. I said, Lord, it's not fair. I told him how bitter I
was that the President should receive this tremendous homecoming, when *no one* met us as we returned
home. And you know, when I finished, it seemed as
though the Lord put his hand on my shoulder and
simply said, *'But you're not home yet!'* "

That's a great truth! There *are* rewards for believers, but not necessarily down here. The rewards here
have to do with the strengthening of the inner life,
not the outer. We must always consider ourselves un-
profitable servants, having done only that which is
our duty to do. We have no claim on God by reason of
our faithful service—it is only what we should have
done. We have no right to come to him in prayer and
demand that he answer because we have done this, or
that, or another thing. Jesus says when a man stands
and lists his accomplishments before God, he is *not
praying.* Is it not possible that after years of praying
we must now realize we have never prayed at all?

Upside-Down Is All Right

Now let's take a look at the publican to see what prayer is. It seems at first that he does it all wrong: He stands afar off; he doesn't even lift his eyes—he fails to assume the proper position of prayer. But how totally unimportant are these externals of prayer! Years ago Sam Walter Foss wrote a poem which says it so well. He called it "The Prayer of Cyrus Brown":

"The proper way for a man to pray,"
Said Deacon Lemuel Keyes,
"And the only proper attitude
Is down upon his knees."

"No, I should say the way to pray,"
Said Reverend Doctor Wise,
"Is standing straight with outstretched arms
And rapt and upturned eyes."

"Oh, no, no, no," said Elder Slow,
"Such posture is too proud.
A man should pray with eyes fast-closed
And head contritely bowed."

"It seems to me his hands should be
Austerely clasped in front
With both thumbs pointing toward the
    ground,"
Said Reverend Doctor Blunt.

"Last year I fell in Hidgekin's well
Headfirst," said Cyrus Brown,
"With both my heels a-stickin' up
And my head a-pointing down.

"And I made a prayer right then and there,
The best prayer I ever said,
The prayingest prayer I ever prayed,
A-standin' on my head."

The publican came into the temple and stood with his eyes cast down. He did not assume the proper posture of prayer; he was not even in the right place; he stood "afar off." All he could do was beat his breast and say, "God be merciful to me a sinner." Someone has called that "a holy telegram." I like that: short, pithy, right to the point—but true prayer.

What do we learn about prayer from *this* man? Isn't it obvious that authentic prayer is *an awareness of our helpless need?* This man saw himself on the lowest possible level, a sinner. In fact, the original language is even stronger: "God be merciful to me *the* sinner"—the sinner, the very lowest, worst kind. He believed that without God he could do *absolutely nothing* to help his position. "I'm a sinner, Lord, that's all I can say; I have nothing else to add."

Note that he doesn't try to add anything by way of merit. He does not say, "God be merciful to me a *penitent* sinner." He *was* penitent, but he doesn't urge that as any basis for God's blessing. Neither does he say, "God be merciful to me a *reformed* sinner. I'm going to be different from now on." I am sure he did do differently—no doubt he stopped his extortion and cheating and his improper reporting, but still he does not refer to himself as "a reformed sinner." Nor does he say, "God be merciful to me an *honest* sinner. Here I am, Lord, willing to tell you the whole thing. Surely you can't pass by honesty like that." In fact, he does not even say, "God be merciful to me a *praying* sinner." He rests his whole case on the merciful character of God and says, in effect, "Lord, I haven't a thing to lean on but you."

This tax collector recognized that there *were* things he could do, activities he could perform, for he had been living on that basis all his life. But also he had come to the realization that doing them again would only be perpetuating the same old sin—that to do *anything* right, even the normal activities of his life, he needed God; he simply *had* to have God!

Judge Upward

How did he come to this place? Exactly the reverse from the way of the Pharisee. He did not look *down* on someone else below him; he looked *up* to God. He judged upward to God. He saw no one but God; he heard the word, "Thou shalt love the Lord thy God with all thy soul and all thy strength and all thy mind," and judged himself on that basis. Lord, I'm *the* sinner. I need mercy. And in taking that place, all that God is becomes available to him.

There is no answer to the awesome problems of juvenile delinquency, immorality, drug-addiction, homosexuality (and all the other terrible, gripping forces that lay hold of human lives today) except for an individual struggling with these to cast himself wholly upon God and say, "I'm a sinner."

Unfortunately, we seem to think that such a commitment is "for emergency use only," when we are up against it and there is nowhere else to turn. We learn so slowly that this is man's *normal* basis of living— that we are always to realize we have no abilities in ourselves. We were never intended to feel adequate to meet any situation apart from Jesus Christ. Prayer, therefore, is an expression of our helplessness, an awareness of need that can be met only by God.

No Other Help

From the publican in our Scripture passage we learn a second thing about true prayer. Authentic prayer is always *an acknowledgement of divine adequacy.* He said, "God be merciful to me," and this is true prayer—whether it be prayer for ourselves in our own

need or prayer for another. Our help must be in God.
This man looked for help nowhere else. He did not
say, "Lord, perhaps this Pharisee standing here can
help me." No, he said, "God be merciful to me." And
in that word "merciful" is hidden all the wonderful
story of the coming of Jesus Christ, the bloody cross,
and the resurrection. This man used a theological
word which means "be propitiated to me," that is,
"Having had your justice satisfied, Lord, now show
me your love." And he *believed* that God's mercy was
his, for Jesus said he went down to his house justified.
He was changed; he was different; he was made
whole. He laid hold of what God said and believed
him. That, too, is what true prayer is.

Prayer is more than asking; prayer is *talking.*
Prayer is more than pleading; prayer is *believing.*
Prayer is more than words uttered; it is *an attitude
maintained.* How many times we ought to be praying!
Whenever there is an awareness of need, that is an opportunity to let the heart, the thought, and the voice
(whatever form prayer may take) lift immediately to
God and say, "God, be merciful. Lord, meet this
need. My hope, my help, my everything is in you for
this moment." It doesn't matter whether it is only
tying your shoes or washing the dishes or writing a
letter or turning out a paper or making a telephone
call. Whenever there's a need, that is the time for
prayer. Prayer is that expression of dependence which
lays hold of God's resources—for any need.

Now, the question I ask of my own heart is this.
Have I ever prayed? Have I *ever* prayed? If what Jesus
says is true—that prayer is the opposite of fainting—
why do I find my life so often filled with fainting, losing heart, discouragement, defeat? The obvious answer is that I have not been really praying, for prayer
and fainting cannot exist together.

This is where Jesus leaves us. Have you ever prayed? Have you ever really prayed? Have you ever launched upon a life of prayer where every moment you are counting on God to meet your need? Will you this day begin that life? Perhaps for the first time you can say, "Lord, be merciful to me, *the* sinner." This is the nature of prayer.

Holy Father, help us to take these words seriously. They are not intended merely to entertain us or even to instruct us, but to change us, to set us free, to make us live, to turn us from weakness and emptiness and barrenness and fruitlessness, to truth and life and joy. We ask now that we may begin to live a life of prayer. We have no other help, but you are fully adequate. On this we rest—in Jesus' name.

He was praying in a certain place, and when he ceased, one of his disciples said to him, "Lord, teach us to pray, as John taught his disciples" (Luke 11:1).

3
HOW JESUS PRAYED

Jesus was a source of continual amazement to his own disciples. Life with him was one unending experience of joy and bewilderment, and they were forever attempting to explain him to their own satisfaction. They had traveled with him the length and breadth of the land of Israel, and it had been like a great military campaign. They saw inroads made into the darkening powers of sickness, death, and despair throughout the land.

The disciples could not forget the mighty demonstrations of his power. They remembered the grateful eyes of the lame, blind, sick, dumb, and deaf—those afflicted ones who had been healed and set free and sent back to their loved ones. They were continually astonished at the wisdom that Jesus manifested and were forever watching him, wondering what was the secret of his wisdom and power. When he was eating, sleeping, teaching, traveling, they were always watching.

In Luke 11:1 we read that Jesus was praying, and when he had ceased, one of his disciples spoke to him. They had been watching him in prayer and suddenly the idea dawned on one of the disciples that somehow the amazing power of Jesus was connected with his prayer life. So speaking for all the disciples, he said, "Lord, teach us to pray."

This is a very significant request, because these disciples were undoubtedly already men of prayer. When they say to him, "Lord, teach us to pray, as John taught his disciples," they do not mean to imply that John had a superior school of ministry. They are not saying, "In that traveling seminary that John conducted he had a course on prayer, but you have not told us anything about this yet." What they mean is, "Some of us once were John's disciples and were taught by him how to pray, but Lord, we have been watching you and we see that you are a master at prayer. Now, as John once taught us how to pray, would you also impart to us the secrets of prayer? For we have seen that in some manner, the marvel and mystery of your character is linked with your prayer life, and it has made us aware of how little we really know about prayer. Lord, would you teach us to pray?"

If there is one prayer more than another that is burning in my own heart, it is that in all simplicity, out of an awareness of our own deep need in this respect, we each might cry out with urgency as did this disciple, "Lord, teach us to pray." For the brutal fact is, we do not know how to pray, either as individuals or as a church. And the proof that we do not know how to pray as individuals is found in the tremendous amount of fainting that is visible in our midst—the discouragement, anxiety, fear, guilt, and despair that is evident in many lives.

Those who have learned something of the strengthening ministry of prayer in the individual life have a joy and a glow in their experience that cannot be denied. There are those who approach every circumstance with that compelling irresistible triumph that marks authentic Christian faith, and in their lives the ministry of prayer is very evident. But we must admit there is much fainting, too, among young and old alike, and this marks the lack of real prayer.

If we who are Christians are failing in this vital area, it is simply because we have not yet seen what prayer is and the part it plays in Christian living. Somehow the enemy has blurred our senses and dimmed our eyes so that we do not see this clearly. Shall we now join this unnamed disciple, and cry, out of desperate, hungry, powerless lives, "Lord, teach us to pray"?

One thing is immediately evident. When we say these words from our hearts, we have already taken the first and most important step toward discovering the power of prayer. When we ask, "Teach us to pray," we do so out of a sense of need. Prayer, as we have seen, is simply the expression of human need to an eager Father—the cry of a beloved child to a Father who is ready to pour out all that he has to give.

We will examine in due course what our Lord said to these disciples in response to this request, but for the present let us be content to ask what they saw in his life that wrenched this cry from their hearts.

What was it that impressed them as they watched Jesus pray? What convinced them that his prayer life and his amazing power and wisdom were somehow related?

The Breath of Life

They saw, first of all, that with Jesus prayer was a necessity. It was more than an occasional practice on his part; it was a lifelong habit. It was an attitude of mind and heart—an atmosphere in which he lived; the very air he breathed. Everything he did arose out of prayer. He literally prayed without ceasing, as the Apostle Paul urges us to do.

Obviously it was not always formal prayer. He did not always kneel or continually stand with bowed head in an attitude of prayer. If he had, of course, he wouldn't have been able to get anything else done.

And it is amazing that he fulfilled his prayer life in the midst of an incredibly busy ministry. It is astonishing how much he crammed into three years. He was subjected, like many of us, to a life of increasing pressure, of continual interruption. As he ministered, he met with growing opposition, with increasing harassment and continual resistance to the course he was taking, even from his own disciples. Yet in the midst of this life of incredible busyness and tremendous pressure and frequent interruption he was constantly in prayer. He was praying in spirit when his hands were busy healing. He gave thanks as he was breaking the bread and feeding the five thousand. He gave thanks to the Father at the tomb of Lazarus before he spoke those words, "Lazarus, come forth" (John 11:43), in that dramatic display of power. When the Greeks came and wanted to see Jesus, his immediate response was one of prayer: "Father, glorify thy name" (John 12:28). There was a continual sense of expectation that the Father would be working through him, and thus, by his attitude, Jesus was praying all the time.

The Son Can Do Nothing . . .

This is the secret of prayer and of the prayer life: Practice this constant expectancy of attitude which means that we are never very far away from the thought that God is working in us both to will and to do of his good pleasure. Jesus did this, of course, because he believed what he preached. He said continually, "The Son can do nothing of his own accord" (John 5:19). Those were not mere words. He was not mouthing pious phrases, as we frequently do, or trying to make a good impression on those around him. He was saying something that startled them, but he meant it, "The Son, by himself, can do nothing." What an amazing thing for him to say!

Think of the Son of God, the perfect Man, who adequately and continually fulfilled all God's expectation for men, who was the constant delight of the Father's heart, who always did those things that pleased him, and ask yourself how much he personally, as a man, contributed to the mighty program of power and wisdom that occupied three years of ministry. The answer is, nothing—absolutely nothing! Again and again he declared that to be true: "The Father who dwells in me does his works" (John 14:10). And out of this conscious, constant sense of need there arose a continuing attitude of prayer, a continuing expectation that if anything was to be done, the Father would have to do it.

Emergency Use Only?

Now, our problem is that we have such an unexplainable attitude of self-sufficiency. Oh, there are times when we are conscious of our inadequacy and our need and are ready for prayer. Whenever you get down in the dumps or come up against some demanding circumstance or are overwhelmed by some unexpected catastrophe, your first and automatic response is prayer, isn't it? Why? Because you have a sense of need. You know you need help, and prayer is an automatic response at such times. We tend to think prayer is only an emergency measure, reserved for those times when we are under great pressure or strain. For the rest of life we feel quite sufficient and say, "I'll pray when I need help, but the rest I can manage on my own."

But the secret of the life of Jesus is that he *never* said that nor even once thought it. He never said to himself, "My training, my background, my knowledge, and the ability that God has given to me as a man make me sufficient for certain things on my own." No, he said, "The Son by himself can do nothing." Absolutely nothing!

The Fishing Expert

On one occasion our Lord was addressing a great crowd on the lakeshore, and as he was speaking, they pressed so closely around him that he could no longer be easily seen or heard (Luke 5:1-8). So he climbed into Peter's boat and told him to move out a bit into the lake. Peter paddled it out a few feet from the shore where the Lord could be seen and heard much better, and he continued his address.

Imagine how Peter must have reacted to this. At last he was able to do something for his Lord. It was his boat, and the Lord was his guest. The Lord had done so much for him that his heart must have rejoiced at this opportunity to provide something that Christ needed and without which he could not have carried on his ministry. But when our Lord finished his discourse that day and dismissed the crowd, he turned and said, "Peter, put out into the deep"; that is, move out into the depths of the lake. When Peter had taken the boat out into the middle of the lake, the Lord said to him, "Now, Peter, cast in your net. Get ready to fish." And Peter looked at the Lord in amazement. You can see the almost incredulous look on his face and hear the patronizing tone in his voice when he replied, "Lord, we have been fishing all night long and caught nothing."

What he was thinking, unquestionably, was something like this: "Lord, I know you are a great teacher. You certainly know how to speak to men far better than I. You are a mighty man of power, a man of incredible wisdom. You obviously know secrets that we know nothing about, but Lord, when it comes to fishing you're talking to an expert. If you want to know anything about fishing, I'll be glad to instruct you. After all, Lord, I have been raised on this lake. I know where there are fish and where there are none. I know when they bite and when they don't. I have been fishing all night long, Lord, and have caught absolutely nothing. Now take my advice, Lord; you stick to your preaching and let me do the fishing."

But the Lord said, "Peter, let down your nets for a catch." And something about his tone was so irresistible that Peter replied, "Nevertheless Lord, at your word I will." So he let down the net and enclosed a great host of fish so large that the net began to break as they drew the fish into the boat. As Peter tumbled them into the bottom of the boat and stood there, knee-deep in fish, he looked up at his Lord with painful surprise and said, "Depart from me, for I am a sinful man, O Lord." What did he mean? He meant,

"Lord, I see what you mean. I see that even in those areas where I think myself to be sufficient I need you."

Surely this is what our Lord is teaching us. This is one thing we must learn: there is no activity of life which does not require prayer, a sense of expectation of God at work. Is not this what that disciple felt (it may even have been Peter) as he watched our Lord praying? He knew that, to him, prayer was an option. He prayed when he felt like it, only when he thought it necessary, thinking that prayer was designed for emergency use only, for the "big" problems of life. But he could see that for Jesus, prayer was an ever present necessity.

We need to begin right where we are . . . the phone call that I am about to make—I can't do it right except in prayer. It will never have the effect it ought to have except as my heart looks up to God and says, "Speak through me in this." The letter I am about to write . . . this part I am making on the machine . . . the interview I am about to conduct . . . the chart I have to make for my studies . . . this report that I must turn in tomorrow . . . the room I am sweeping . . . that walk I am going to take . . . the game I am about to play. How can I do these things right and fulfill my ministry except as I look to you, Lord, to do it through me? These are the unending needs from which prayer rises.

Someone asked a dear cleaning lady what her method of prayer was, and she said, "I don't know nothin' about method. I just pray like this: When I wash my clothes, I pray, Lord, wash my heart clean. When I iron them I say, Lord, iron out all these troubles I can't do nothin' about. When I sweep the floor, I say, Lord, sweep all the corners of my life like I'm sweepin' this floor." That is real prayer.

The second thing this disciple saw in Jesus was that prayer was not only necessary but it was also perfectly natural. There was no struggle on his part to pray—no driving of himself. Prayer to him was not an act of self-discipline or duty, it was always delight.

Now, that does not mean that our Lord did not require time for prayer nor that he did not have to arrange for prayer in his program. He had to make choices between other demanding things that threatened to usurp his time. Sometimes he spent hours and even whole nights in prayer. Occasionally he slipped away when the crowds were the very largest and making the most demands upon him. Luke records in this same Gospel that a great multitude came together to hear him, but he withdrew himself to a desert place and prayed (Luke 5:16).

Certainly there were times when he was weary and pressed and prayer was not the easiest thing to do under the circumstances. That time in Gethsemane's garden he must have been, like the disciples, weary and sleepy, emotionally and physically exhausted, but as they slept, he prayed. Yet it was no apparent problem to our Lord. There was no sense of reluctance or that this was a requirement he had to fulfill. He never seemed to drag himself away from something else to pray.

Why not? Because, again, his actions arose out of an overwhelming sense of need. He simply faced up to the fact that without this relationship what he did was wasted time. He could put in hours of activity but it accomplished nothing. And out of that deep, urgent sense of continual need, that awareness that he was but an empty channel—a vessel through whom the Father worked—there arose his continual prayer.

This is what we must come to, isn't it? We urgently require a sense of need! Offer a sandwich to a man who is stuffed with a heavy dinner and you will have to use all your powers of persuasion to get him to accept it. And if he does, it will only be out of politeness, and as soon as your back is turned he will dispose of it behind the sofa. Why? Because he has no sense of need. Though he may feel a duty to accept it, he does not want it and it is of no value to him. But try offering just one sandwich to a hungry teenage boy. You had better start making another one as soon as he takes the first! So, prayer to Jesus was as necessary as eating and just as natural.

Thank You, Father

Sometimes for Jesus it meant thanksgiving. You have such a prayer in Luke 10:

> *In that same hour he rejoiced in the Holy Spirit and said, "I thank thee, Father, Lord of heaven and earth, that thou hast hidden these things from the wise and understanding and revealed them to babes; yea, Father, for such was thy gracious will. All things have been delivered to me by my Father; and no one knows who the Son is except the Father, or who the Father is except the Son and any one to whom the Son chooses to reveal him" (Luke 10:21, 22).*

He was always giving thanks. He was forever saying, "Thank you, Father. Thank you for the circumstance into which you have brought me, thank you for what you have planned to do about it, thank you for the victory that will be won through these circumstances, thank you for the needs that are being met." As he broke the bread to feed the five thousand, he lifted his eyes and said, "Thank you, Father." At the Last Supper, as he gathered with his own in the upper room, he took the cup and when he had *given thanks* he said, "Take, eat." Throughout all of his life, prayer was thanksgiving.

Sometimes prayer was seeking counsel from the Father. On the occasion when he was about to choose his disciples we are told he spent all the previous night in prayer (Luke 6:12, 13). What was he doing? He was seeking and receiving illumination and guidance from the Father. He knew his own wisdom would be inadequate for this task. He simply exposed himself to the divine counsel of the Father, and together they went down the list and talked over every single man. As he talked with the Father about each one, there came a conviction to his heart, "This is the one," and when he had finished, he chose the twelve, including Judas.

Prayer for Jesus was also frequently intercession. We have the great example of it in John 17—that mighty prayer in which he prayed for the eleven apostles and through them for the whole church to every succeeding age. "I pray not for the world," he said, "but I pray for these and those who will hear my word through them." He prayed for Peter in the hour of his disillusionment and defeat when his world came crashing around his head in the dark, dark night when he denied his Lord and went out and wept bitterly. The Lord had met him before and said, "Peter, I have prayed for you that your faith may not fail" (Luke 22:32). Both Judas and Peter denied their Lord that night, but the fundamental difference between Judas and Peter was that Christ had prayed for Peter.

He prayed for the little children and made intercession for them with the Father. And finally, his great prayer of intercession was prayed on the bloody

cross when his arms were stretched out. He prayed as
they hammered the nails home in his flesh, "Father,
forgive them; for they know not what they do" (Luke
23:34).

And then, supremely, prayer was communion to
Jesus. He prayed on the Mount of Transfiguration,
and as his disciples watched him, he was suddenly
transformed before them. *"As he was praying,"* the
countenance of his face was altered and his garments
became white and shining. In prayer he was experiencing a communion so rich that the glory of the
Father which dwelt within him broke through the
tent in which it was hidden. As John says, "We have
beheld his glory, glory as of the only Son from the
Father" (John 1:14).

Jesus prayed in the Garden and experienced real
communion in an hour of deep anguish of heart, and
was then strengthened by an angel who ministered to
him in the midst of the pressures that he faced. And
so as we trace through the prayer life of Jesus, we can
see that prayer was so necessary to him, so easy, so
natural.

Who Said That?

Why do we struggle so, then? Why are we suddenly so busy when the prayer meeting is brought
up? Why do we piously favor prayer in general and
devilishly resist it in particular? Perhaps even now
the enemy is whispering two very clever things to us
about prayer. Is he saying something like this: "Of
course Jesus prayed like this, but do you expect to
live like he did? Do you really think that you can live
on the level of the Son of God? Isn't it obvious that
this kind of living is far beyond you? After all, you are
nothing but a simple, ordinary Christian."

Like everything else the devil says to us, that is a
filthy lie, because the Lord Jesus says, *"As I live by the*

Father, even so shall you live by me. As the Father has sent me, even so send I you." As he lived by the Father's strength, so we are to live by the Son's strength in exactly the same relationship.

Or perhaps the enemy is saying to us, "Well, Jesus prayed as he did because he felt a sense of need continually. It is easy to pray, you know, when you feel need. So go ahead and pray when you need to. But don't bother unless you feel a sense of need." That is another slimy word that speaks for what has become a widespread philosophy of prayer, which is, follow your feelings. In other words, don't bother to walk by faith.

Faith reckons on fact, and the fact that God reveals to us is that *whether we sense need or not, we are needy.* Whether we feel insufficient or not, *we are insufficient.* We are continually needy and we must reckon momentarily and constantly on the indwelling life of the Lord Jesus within us for strength. When we think that everything is fine, that we need no help from God and that life is under control, we are suffering from a satanic delusion, a fantasy, a soap bubble of imagination which is bound ultimately to burst in slippery confusion.

Life is really under control only when our attitude is what Jesus' attitude was: one of continual need and constant expectation. God is always the same, and on that great unshakeable rock, faith continually rests. Giving is his job, ours is to receive. Prayer, then, is to be our life and our breath so that no one need urge us to pray any more than they would urge us to breathe or to eat. We *know* we must pray.

Once, when I was standing in the Lincoln Memorial in Washington, D.C., I read again those amazing words engraved on the walls—Lincoln's Gettysburg Address and, on the other side, his Second

Inaugural Address. The words of the Second Inaugural came home to me with tremendous impact. It is more like a sermon than a political speech.

I remembered that when Lincoln entered the Presidency he was not a Christian, as he himself said. But as the burdens of that great office devolved upon him and the crushing responsibility and sorrow of the war gripped his heart, he said that while he was walking among the graves of the soldiers at Gettysburg, there burst upon him an awareness of his need of the Savior. Later he testified that it was there he became a Christian.

Lincoln learned to pray, and for him the purpose of prayer was not to get God to do man's bidding, but to enable man to see God's purposes and to experience the strength of relying on the everlasting arms. Lincoln left this testimony about prayer: "I have been driven many times to my knees by the overwhelming conviction that I had absolutely no other place to go." In the strength of that continual reliance upon God he became our nation's greatest president.

> *Father, what can we say in this hour but to cry out as these disciples cried out, Lord, teach us to pray. Teach us our need. Tear away this veil from our eyes that makes us think we have any adequacy in ourselves. Deliver us from this satanic delusion, this widespread worldly philosophy that our knowledge, our education, our training can provide an adequate background for activity. Give us rather this conscious sense of dependence, this ~ness that nothing that we do will be of any ~art from a dependence upon you. In Jesus' ~en.*

"When the unclean spirit has gone out of a man, he passes through waterless places seeking rest; and finding none he says, 'I will return to my house from which I came'" (Luke 11:24).

4

THE PATTERN
OF PRAYER

We have observed the prayer life of our Lord Jesus in Luke 11:1 through the eyes of an unnamed disciple who was watching him pray. As we looked together at Jesus' praying, I hope a dawning conviction stole over you, as it did over this unnamed disciple, that prayer was the secret of this amazing life and that it was both the most natural and most necessary aspect of Jesus' existence. I hope, too, that you heard within yourself the urgent cry of this disciple, "Lord, teach us to pray."

In answer to that request, Jesus gave his disciples what is called the model prayer. We have a very brief account of it in Luke 11:

> *And he said to them, "When you pray, say:*
> *Father, hallowed be thy name. Thy kingdom*
> *come. Give us each day our daily bread; and for-*
> *give us our sins, for we ourselves forgive every one*
> *who is indebted to us; and lead us not into tempta-*
> *tion" (Luke 11:2-4).*

This is slightly different from the more familiar form in Matthew which was undoubtedly spoken on a different occasion (Matthew 6:9-13) (Jesus frequently repeated certain great truths during his ministry). In either form, the Lord's Prayer is large enough and great enough to encompass the whole of our lives. It is like a mighty rainbow that spans our years from birth to death and gathers up into one all the varied colors of our lives.

This prayer falls into two rather obvious divisions, highlighted by the use of two pronouns. The first part centers on God, using the pronoun "thy." "Hallowed be thy name. Thy kingdom come." The second part concerns man, and here the pronoun "us" occurs. "Give us our daily bread; forgive us our sins; lead us not into temptation." For now, we are going to confine ourselves to those first three phrases that center around the person, character, and being of God.

It is no accident, I am sure, that in prayer as in everything else, Jesus invariably puts the things concerning God first. Surely this exposes a fatal weakness in our own prayers, which so frequently begin with us. We rush almost immediately into a series of pleading petitions that have to do with *our* problems and *our* irritations. This only serves to focus our attention upon what is already troubling us and to increase our awareness of our lack. Perhaps that is the reason we frequently end up more depressed or more frustrated than when we began.

As a Child

But Jesus shows us another way. We must begin with God. We must take a slow, calm, reassuring gaze at him—at his greatness and his eagerness to give, his unwearied patience and untiring love. Then, of course, the first thing we receive in prayer is a calm spirit, and there is no need for us to plunge into a panicky flood of words.

This is why this pattern prayer begins with a word of relationship, "Father." May I point out that it is "Father," not "Old Man"! There is a reverence about the word "father" that is totally absent in some modern expressions of fatherhood, and surely this is the attitude our Lord intends for us to capture as we begin our study in this prayer.

It is essential to know to whom we are praying. When we come to prayer, we are not talking *about* God. We are not engaging in a theological dialogue. We are talking *with* God. And since we are going to converse with him directly, it is essential that we understand to whom we are speaking. Our Lord gathers it all up in this marvelously expressive word and says true prayer must begin with a concept of God as Father.

Immediately, that eliminates a number of other concepts. It shows us that prayer, real prayer, is never to be addressed to The Chairman of the Committee for Welfare and Relief. Sometimes our prayers take on that aspect. We come expecting a handout. We want something to be poured into our laps, something we think we need, and in making an appeal we are only filling out the properly prescribed forms.

Nor is prayer addressed to The Chief of the Bureau of Investigation. Prayer is never to be merely a confession of our wrongdoings, with the hope that we may cast ourselves upon the mercy of the court. Nor is it an appeal to The Secretary of the Treasury, some sort of genial international banker whom we hope to interest in financing our projects. Rather, prayer is to a Father with a father's heart, a father's love, and a father's strength. The first and truest note of prayer must be our recognition that we come to this kind of father. We must hear him and come to him as a child, in trust and simplicity and with all the frankness of a child—otherwise it is not prayer.

Someone has pointed out that the word "father" answers all the philosophical questions about the nature of God. A father is a person; therefore, God is not a blind force behind the inscrutable machinery of the universe. A father is able to hear; therefore, God is not some impersonal being, aloof from all our troubles and problems. And above all, a father is predisposed by his love and relationship to give a careful, attentive ear to what his child says. God is this way. From a father a child can surely expect a reply.

Our Lord goes on to teach us more of what a father is like in the parable that follows this prayer. The power of it is surely that God is interested in what we have to say. A father, therefore, may be expected to reply to us.

We are not only to address God as "Father"; that is, simply saying the word with our lips, but we are to believe that he *is* a Father, for all that God makes available to mankind must always come to us through faith, must always operate in our lives through belief. Belief invariably involves an actual commitment of the will, a moving of the deepest part of our heart. Belief is *not* expressed by addressing God as "Almighty God" or "Dreadful Creator" or "Ground of all Being"; this betrays our fatal ignorance or unbelief. The greatest authority on prayer says that God is a father!

Someone has suggested that we can combine the extremes of theological persuasion evident in our country today with this prayer: "May the Ground of all Being bless you real good." Such a prayer is absurd, of course. When I come home I do not want my children to meet me in awe and say, "Oh thou great and dreadful Pastor of Peninsula Bible Church, welcome home." It would be an insult to my father-heart. I want my children to greet me as a father. It is never prayer until we recognize that we are coming to a patient and tender father. That is the first note in true prayer.

Dark Closets

The second note of true prayer is one of surrender: "Hallowed be thy name." I am quite sure this is the petition that makes hypocrites out of most of us. We may be able to say "Father" with grateful sincerity, but when we pray, "Hallowed be thy name," we say this with the guilty knowledge that there are areas of our life in which his name is not hallowed, and in which, furthermore, we don't want it to be hallowed.

When we say "Hallowed be thy name," we are praying, "May the whole of my life be a source of delight to you and may it be an honor to the name which I bear, which is your name. Hallowed be your name." We find the same thing in that prayer of David's at the close of one of his great psalms: "Let the words of my mouth and the meditation of my heart be acceptable in thy sight, O LORD, my rock and my redeemer" (Psalm 19:14).

The trouble is that we so frequently know there are great areas of our lives that are not hallowed. There are certain monopolies which we have reserved to ourselves, privileged areas which we do not wish to surrender, where the name of our boss or the name of

our girl-friend or some other dear one means more to
us than the name of God.

But when we pray, "Hallowed be thy name," if
there is any degree whatsoever of sincerity or open-
ness or honestness, we are really praying, "Lord, I
open to you every closet; I am taking every skeleton
out for you to examine. Hallowed be thy name."
There cannot be any contact with God, any real
touching of his power, any genuine experiencing of
the glorious fragrance and wonder of God at work in
human life until we truly pray "Hallowed be thy
name."

But we are not only aware that in each of us there
are areas where God's name is not hallowed, where he
cannot write his name, but furthermore, we are
deeply aware that none of us by ourselves can make
our lives wholly consecrated to God. No matter how
we may try to arrange every area of our lives to please
him, there is a fatal weakness, a flaw that somehow
makes us miss the mark.

But you will notice that this prayer is not phrased
as simply a confession or an expression of repentance
to the Father. We are not to pray as we so frequently
do, "Father, help me to be good," or "Help me to be
better." Isn't it rather remarkable that throughout
this whole pattern prayer not once is a desire for help
in the sanctification of life expressed? That which is
so much our concern and so much the concern of
Scripture is never once reflected in this prayer.

No, Jesus turns our attention entirely away from
ourselves to the Father. This phrase, "Hallowed be
thy name," is really a cry of helpless trust, in which
we are simply standing and saying, "Father, not only
do I know that there are areas in my life where your
name is not hallowed, but I know also that only you
can hallow them. I am quite willing to simply stand

still and let you be the Holy One who will actually be first in my life."

When we pray that way, then we discover that the rest comes by itself, so to speak. The man who lets God be his Lord and surrenders to him is drawn quite spontaneously into a great learning process and becomes a different person. Martin Luther once said, "You do not command a stone which is lying in the sun to be warm. It will be warm all by itself."

When we say, "Father, there is no area of my life that I'm not willing to let you talk to me about, there is no area that I will hide from you: my sexual life, my business life, my social life, my school life, my recreation times, my vacation period"—*that* is saying, "Hallowed be thy name." When we pray that way, we discover that God will walk into the dark closets of our life where the odor is sometimes too much even for us to stand and clean them out and straighten them up and make them fit for his dwelling. "If we walk in the light," John says (and that is not sinlessness: that means where God sees everything), "as he is in the light, we have fellowship with one another, and the blood of Jesus his Son cleanses us from all sin" (1 John 1:7).

How Does Thy Kingdom Come?

The third cry of true prayer, again concerned with God, is a cry of hope, "Thy kingdom come." Now, this can be a sigh for heaven. Who does not get homesick for heaven once in awhile, longing to be free from the desultory humdrumness of life and to experience the glory we read of in the Bible. Or this can be, as it ought to be, a cry for heaven to come to earth. That is, may the kingdoms of this world become the kingdom of our Lord and of his Christ. This is what is expressed in the hymn,

Jesus shall reign where'er the sun
Does his successive journeys run;
His kingdom stretch from shore to shore,
Till moons shall wax and wane no more.

There is much in Scripture about this, and all of us
long for that day to come when God shall rule in
righteousness over all the earth.

But I think this prayer is more than that. It is more
than a long, wistful look into the future, whether on
earth or off earth. It is a cry that God's will may be
done through, and by means of, the blood and sweat
and tears of life, right now. That is, "Thy kingdom
come through what I am going through at this very
moment."

Scripture reveals to us a truth that we could never
know by ourselves, but which becomes self-evident
as we look at life through the lenses of the Word of
God. That is, God, in a manner of speaking, builds
his kingdom in secret. When it is least evident that
he is at work, this is often the time when he is accomplishing the most. Behind the scaffolding of tragedy
and despair, God frequently is erecting his empire of
love and glory. When we think God is silent, and we
feel abandoned; when we feel God has removed his
hand and we no longer sense the friendship of his
presence, God frequently is accomplishing the greatest things of all.

Building Materials

I once talked with a young man who had gone
through a fearsome accident which had left a physical
mark upon him, but in reality a broken marriage had
caused an even deeper scar. He had been raised in a
church environment and before some of these things
took place his outlook had been one of self-righteous
judgment of others, a sort of pious disdain for those

who could not keep free from troubles or problems. But he said, "You know, the humiliation of my divorce cut the ground right out from under my self-righteous attitude. I know that I never would have come to my present joy and understanding of God's purpose if I had not become a divorce statistic." It is in these ways that God builds his kingdom.

What a glorious mystery this is!

> *God moves in a mysterious way*
> *His wonders to perform;*
> *He plants His footsteps in the sea,*
> *And rides upon the storm.*
>
> *Ye fearful saints, fresh courage take;*
> *The clouds ye so much dread*
> *Are filled with mercies, and shall break*
> *In blessings 'round thy head.*

Is there any liturgy or ritual of the church that says this more eloquently to us than the Lord's Supper? When we gather for the breaking of bread and the drinking of wine, we remember that each is a symbol of the pain, anguish, and sorrow of the bitter, bitter death that our Lord went through. But, as Cowper writes,

> *Deep in unfathomable mines*
> *Of never-failing skill*
> *He treasures up His bright designs,*
> *And works His sovereign will.*

Out of darkness God calls forth light; out of despair, hope. From death comes resurrection. You cannot have resurrection without death, hope without despair, or light without darkness. By means of defeat the kingdom of God is born in human hearts.

This is what this prayer means: "Oh, Lord, I am but a little child. I do not understand the mysteries of life. I do not know thy ways in the world of men, but Lord, I pray that through these very circumstances in which I now find myself, through these present troubles, these struggles, thy kingdom come." The transmuting element is prayer—simple, child-like, trustful, rising out of the helpless need of a child to touch a father's heart.

> *Father, how frequently we misunderstand life even though you have been at such great lengths to show us the secret of it. How many times, Father, have we rebelled foolishly against you and your workings in our lives? How many times have we turned away in disgust or despair? And yet, have we not also seen that through these hours of resentment and burning shame and bitterness, you have been at work in love to teach us the truth and to bring us to an understanding of reality, to bring us back to your loving heart? Father, hallowed be thy name. Thy kingdom come. In Jesus' name, Amen.*

"Give us each day our daily bread; and forgive us our sins, for we ourselves forgive every one who is indebted to us; and lead us not into temptation" (Luke 11:3-4).

5
WHEN PRAYER BECOMES PERSONAL

Now we come to the part of our Lord's model prayer that directly concerns us—this last section which takes in the whole experience of life. This is a prayer for the whole of man—body, soul, and spirit. With magnificent accuracy, Jesus puts his finger squarely on the paramount need in each of these areas, so that if we understand this prayer properly, and pray it as it should be prayed, there is really nothing further to be said. One of the amazing things about the Bible is how the writers of Scripture are able to reduce to the simplest terms some of these mighty themes of life, stating them in just a word or two, so that we can grasp what they mean.

As we will see, however, this prayer is not intended to be merely repeated over and over in some mechanical rote-fashion, like a christianized prayer-wheel. Rather, it is intended to become a guide; each of these short phrases is infinitely expandable as to detail. But in principle, this is a completely adequate prayer.

God Likes Bodies

Jesus begins this section of the prayer with the needs of the body. I like that! I find that we have such distorted concepts of prayer that we often feel there is something wrong with praying about physical needs. I am afraid that is a reflection of a pagan concept of life. The Greeks regarded the body as coarse and unworthy of redemption, and they therefore mistreated it. They tortured and tormented their bodies. This idea that the body must be subdued by physical torment or suffering is widespread in the Orient today, but you never find this in the New Testament nor in true Christian faith.

Oh, I know there is that verse in Philippians, which, in the King James Version, speaks of looking for "the Lord Jesus Christ; Who shall change our *vile* body" (Philippians 3:21), but in reality that is a very vile translation! The word does not mean "vile" at all. It means a body of lowliness, of humiliation—that is, not yet glorified. It has not yet entered into the ultimate state that God designs for it. But Paul is not saying there is anything wrong with the body.

It is important to understand that prayer must quite properly continue on this level. God likes bodies. That may startle you, but it is true that God engineered and designed them, and he likes them. It is perfectly proper then that we pray about the needs of the body. Bread, as expressed in the prayer, is a symbol of all the necessities of physical life; it stands for all that our physical life demands—shelter, drink, clothing—anything the body requires.

The vital concern here is that an immediate and unbroken supply be made available to us. The only limit in this prayer is that we are never to pray for a warehouse, a full supply for a year ahead. There are no "giant economy packages" available to us in this area of life. We are to pray for one day's supply.

Now, I would like to put this simply to your own heart as I ask my own: Do you pray daily for your physical needs? I wonder if anyone really does this. Do we pray about the supply of our food, clothing, shelter, and all the physical necessities of life? Do we take time to ask God for them, or at least to give thanks for them? Perhaps this has become such a familiar request in the repeating of the Lord's Prayer that it has lost any real meaning for us and we do not take it seriously. It may be that this is the most flagrant and frequent area of Christian disobedience. For after all, our Lord meant it when he told us to pray, "give us *each day* our daily bread."

Oh, you say, I pray before every meal. Yes, so do I, but unfortunately I find that it is often so perfunctory, so mechanical, that it really sounds like a sanctimonious way of saying, "Let's eat." When I was in high school in Montana, we had a neighbor who was a self-confessed atheist, a godless fellow, but with a very engaging personality. We boys often went out to his place because he was a very generous man and let us do many interesting things on his ranch, but he had no use for the gospel or for Christian things.

At mealtime he engaged in a form of ribald mockery in this matter of giving thanks, and I think he did it to shock us. He would sit down to the table and before anyone could start to eat, he would say, "Now we are going to say grace." "Pass the bread and pass the meat. Pitch in, you gol-darn fools, and eat." Of course he intended it as mockery, but I wonder if our own graces, repeated mechanically, are not equally as blasphemous? I don't wish to be negative at this point, but I am sure that there must have been some good reason why the Lord told us to pray in this particular way.

There may be those who will argue that Jesus said elsewhere, "Your Father knows what you need before you ask him" (Matthew 6:8), so the purpose of this prayer is not to inform God of our needs. And there are others who say it really makes little difference whether they pray about physical things or not because they receive the necessities of life regardless. And there are many people who never bother to pray at all but who are eating steak and ice cream while we Christians are trying to get along on hamburgers and jello. So, what's the point, then, of praying?

We Need the Prayer

The answer to that question really touches the central value of prayer. It is very illuminating. Obviously, prayer is not something by which we inform God of our needs or influence him. But prayer is designed to influence us. It is *we* who are in need of this kind of prayer, not God. Of course he knows what we have need of, for he knows everything about us. But prayer is something *we* need. God does not need to be told; we need to tell him, that is the point.

To understand why this is true, ask yourself what happens when you neglect to pray for, and thank God for, your daily needs. I think if you are honest and examine your life over an extended period of time, you will see that, inevitably, a slow and subtle change occurs in your heart. What happens is that we begin to take these things for granted and gradually succumb to the foolish delusion that we actually can provide these necessities ourselves. We become possessed with the incredible vanity that *our* wisdom and *our* abilities have really made these things possible, that we *can* supply them quite apart from God. And when we begin to think that way, pride swells within us and a kind of blindness settles upon us—a blindness which darkens our spiritual insight, and we become moody, restless, and depressed.

The Book of Daniel describes vividly this type of thinking in the story of Nebuchadnezzar, that proud monarch of Babylon. He walked out in the evening hours upon the battlements of his palace, looked out over the city, and said, "Is not this great Babylon, which I have built by *my* mighty power . . . for the glory of *my* majesty?" (Daniel 4:30). He revelled in what he thought were his powers, inherent in himself, by which all this came to pass.

As a result of that defiant assumption of the basic powers of supply in his life, God brought upon him the judgment of bestiality. He became a beast, and was turned out to grass to eat in the fields like an animal. This was simply God's dramatic way of saying that ingratitude causes men to become animal-like, with all the ferocity and self-centeredness of a beast growling over his food.

Just Like a Dog

I remember Dr. H. A. Ironside telling of an occasion when, as a young man, he went into a cafeteria to eat. When he took his tray and looked around for some place to sit down, he found that all the seats in the room were taken except for one chair opposite a man already seated at a table. Dr. Ironside approached the table and asked if he might sit down. The man looked up, nodded his head, and grunted something unintelligible. So Dr. Ironside sat down and, as was his custom, bowed his head and silently gave thanks for his food. When he looked up, he saw the man eyeing him with a glowering expression. The fellow asked, "What's the matter, something wrong with your food?" Dr. Ironside said, "No, I don't think so, it seems all right to me."

The man persisted: "Have you got a headache, or something?" And Ironside said, "No, I haven't. Why do you ask?"

"Well, I noticed you bowing down and putting your hand up to your head and closing your eyes. I thought maybe there was something wrong with your head." "No," Dr. Ironside replied, "I was simply returning thanks to God for my food."

The man snorted derisively and said, "Oh, you believe in that bosh, do you?" Countering with a question, Dr. Ironside asked, "Don't you ever give thanks?" And the stranger responded, "No, I don't believe in giving thanks for anything. I just start right in." Closing the conversation, Dr. Ironside responded, "Oh, you're just like my dog. He never gives thanks, either, he just starts right in."

After all, it *is* we who need to give thanks to God; it is *we* who must always be reminding ourselves that everything we have comes from his hand and that at any moment he can turn it off if he chooses to do so. It is only by his grace and goodness that our daily needs flow unhindered to us. The only way, therefore, that we can avoid this terrible sin of ingratitude is to pray daily, remembering that

> *Back of the bread is the snowy flour*
> *And back of the flour, the mill*

And back of the mill is the field of wheat,
The rain, and the Father's will.

The second request of the Lord's Prayer moves into the area of human relationships, our conscious life, our emotions, intellect, and will—in other words, the soul of man. Immediately our Lord touches upon the central thing in this area of life, forgiveness: "Forgive us our sins, for we ourselves forgive every one who is indebted to us."

Here is the need for a cleansed conscience, for a sense of peace, of rest with God and man. This is the arena where the emotional clutter of our life takes a very deadly toll. Who of us has not experienced something of the painful results of imagined illnesses? Not that they are really imaginary, for they are physical symptoms that come from a disarrangement of our emotional life. Familiar to all of us are such symptoms as palpitations of the heart, flutterings, shortness of breath (sometimes called "air-hunger"), skin rashes, throbbing migraine headaches that seem to split the skull, stammering, stuttering, nervous compulsions, and a whole host of vague, undefined reactions that we tend to pass off lightly as the "flim-flams," the "heebie-jeebies," or the "squizzels." And then there are the really troublesome mental symptoms: morbid depressions, unreasoning fears and insecurity, and so on. Where do all these grinning demons come from?

Both Scripture and modern psychology agree that underneath these symptoms lurk two frightening monsters: fear and guilt. If we can find a way to slay these fiery dragons, the whole emotional atmosphere of our life will be at peace. And in this simple prayer that Jesus gives us we find a mighty sword. When we pray, "Forgive us our sins," we are asking for the reality that God promises to every believer in Jesus Christ, "There is therefore now no condemnation for those who are in Christ Jesus" (Romans 8:1).

I don't know of anything that troubles Christians more than a sense of guilt. Guilt is the most frequent problem behind the distressing ailments evident in many a Christian's experience, but in this simple prayer is found a fully adequate answer. For if we have laid hold of the forgiveness of God, we know there is nothing any longer between us and the Lord. Our hearts are absolutely free before him and the result is a pervading sense of peace.

But notice now, Jesus immediately adds a limitation to this. As in the realm of the physical, we could pray only about this day's needs, so here we cannot ask God to "forgive us our sins" unless we are willing and *have said* to others that they are forgiven for their trespasses against us.

There doesn't need to be any confusion at this point. Jesus is certainly not referring here to that divine forgiveness that accompanies conversion. The Lord's Prayer is meant for Christians—for only Christians can really pray it intelligently. No non-Christian ever receives forgiveness from God on the basis of how he forgives everyone else. It is simply impossible for him to forgive until he himself has first received the forgiveness of God, and that forgiveness is offered on the basis of the death of Jesus.

Paul says, "In him we have redemption through his blood, the forgiveness of our trespasses, according to the riches of his grace" (Ephesians 1:7). Grace, that's all. We come thanking him for what Jesus' death on the cross has already done in taking away the awful burden of our sin. But, though we have received that forgiveness, we will never be able to enjoy forgiveness from the defilements of our Christian walk unless we are ready to extend it freely to those who offend us. Such forgiveness keeps us enjoying unbroken fellowship with the Father and with the Son, which is, of course, the secret of emotional quietness and rest.

Jesus is simply saying that as a Christian there is no use praying, "Father, forgive my sins," if you are holding a grudge against someone else, or are burning with resentment, filled with bitterness, or are eating your heart out over some real or fancied slight that has come to you. Our instructions are clear: "First be reconciled to your brother, and then come and offer your gift" (Matthew 5:24).

Forgive your brother, and then the healing forgiveness of God will flood your own heart. You will find then that nothing can destroy the God-given peace down at the very center of your being. If we refuse to forgive someone else, we are really withholding from another the grace that has already been shown to us. It is only because we have already been forgiven the great and staggering debt of our own sins that we can ever find the grace to forgive the relatively insignificant slights someone else has heaped upon us.

A man once said to me, "I know that I am a Christian, but someone did an awful thing to me, and I can't forget or forgive him." I replied, "Are you sure that you can't forgive him?" He maintained that he had really tried to forgive this man, but was unable to do so.

Continuing, I said, "You know, I have discovered that we often use the word 'can't' when what we really mean is 'won't.' Isn't it possible that what you are saying is not, 'I can't forgive,' but 'I won't forgive him'? If it is really true that you cannot forgive this man, then it indicates that you yourself have never been forgiven and you are only kidding yourself about being a Christian." This shook him a bit. He thought it through and then, with rather a sheepish grin, he said, "I guess you're right. I guess it is 'won't.'" It was not long, then, before he was able truly to forgive the man who had injured him.

If we take these words seriously, what a revolution this will make in our lives, in our homes, and in our churches. We will never discover what God means in terms of the sweetness of forgiving grace in our own lives and hearts if we are not willing to melt the black frost of years that has withered our relationships with others. When we are ready to forgive others, this great grace is ours as well.

The third area of prayer is in the realm of the spirit: "Lead us not into temptation." Again, the vital core of the matter is touched. In the unseen war of the spirit the greatest needs of our lives are deliverance and protection. But an immediate problem arises here, for Scripture reveals that temptation is necessary to us and no one escapes it in the Christian life. Furthermore, though God himself never tempts us to sin, yet he does test us with difficult and discouraging circumstances and these become the instruments of God to strengthen us, to build us up and give us victory.

When we read this portion of the Lord's Prayer, we are confronted with this question: Are we really expected to pray that God will not do what he must do to accomplish his work within us? After all, even Jesus, we are told, was led by the Spirit into the wilderness to be tempted by the devil. What then does he mean, "Lead us not into temptation"?

Unrecognized Temptation

I confess that over the years I have puzzled and prayed and read about this. But now I am convinced that what Jesus meant is that we should pray to be kept from *unrecognized temptation.* When temptation is recognized, it can be resisted, and when we resist, it is always a source of strength and growth in our lives. If I am filling out my income tax and find that some income has come to me through other than ordinary channels and there is no way of anyone checking it, I am confronted with a temptation to omit it. But I know that is wrong. No one has to tell me; I know it. And when I resist that, I find I am stronger the next time when even a larger amount may be involved.

You see, it is a rather simple matter to resist obvious evil, if we really mean to walk with God. But temptation is not always so easily discerned. There are times when I feel sure I am right and with utmost sincerity and integrity of heart do what I believe is the right thing, but later I look back and see that I was tragically and horribly wrong. That is what Jesus is talking about in this part of the prayer.

Peter is an example of this. In the Upper Room, with brash confidence and utter naïveté, Peter said to the Lord, "Though others forsake you, I will never forsake you." He walked out of that room with these words of our Lord ringing in his ears, "Peter, before this night is over, before the cock crows in the morning, you will have denied me three times" (Matthew 26:33-35).

Still confident, Peter went into the Garden of Gethsemane, and when the soldiers came, he struck off the ear of the high priest's servant in his eagerness to show his faithfulness to the Lord. Earlier Jesus had said to him in the garden, "Peter, watch and pray *that you may not enter into temptation*" (Matthew 26:41). But Peter didn't heed that word. Instead he slept, and after waking him our Lord again asked him to pray— not for the Lord, but for himself.

But Peter did not pray, and when he came into the court of the high priest and was standing before the fire, Satan took him and wrung his courage out like a dishrag and hung him up, limp, to dry, in the presence of a little girl. There, with cursing and swearing, he found himself trapped. Then he denied his Lord, and in the awful realization of what he had done, Peter went out into the blackness of the night and wept bitterly.

This is what our Lord refers to in the phrase, "Lead us not into temptation." This prayer is the recognition of our foolish weakness and our tendency to stumble on into blind folly. It is what we desperately need to pray.

There is a story out of the life of Hudson Taylor, that intrepid missionary to the inland of China, that graphically illustrates this need. When he was only a young man, earnestly trying to do the will of God in China, he journeyed from Swatow up to the great city of Shanghai. There Mr. Taylor planned to get his medical instruments and medicines and return with them to the city of Swatow where he expected to labor with a Scottish missionary who had formerly been his companion there.

When he arrived in Shanghai, he discovered to his tremendous disappointment and chagrin that the building in which he had left all his medical supplies and instruments had been burned to the ground and everything was destroyed. Vexed and puzzled, he sat down to think of what he could do. He had hardly any money, but he decided to beat his way down the network of canals to the city of Ningpo where he could buy some supplies from another missionary, and then take a boat back to Swatow. It was a terribly hot summer, and in the awful heat of those days he worked his way down the canal, preaching as he went.

When Mr. Taylor came to the end of the canals, he had to engage coolies to carry his baggage. After hiring one group of coolies, he started out ahead, but at a given point he had to wait through a long, hot afternoon for them to catch up. To his dismay he discovered when they finally arrived that they were all opium-smokers and would be unable to carry the load over the distance ahead. So he dismissed them, and leaving the chief coolie to hire another group, he started out once more. But this time he never saw the coolies or his baggage again. There were rumors that they had taken the baggage and headed for the hills. Completely discouraged and hardly knowing what to do, he went into an inn to try to get some sleep and found it a rat-infested, bedbug-infested place where he spent a miserable night.

The next morning he decided to press on to the coast and, after a long, hot, and terribly discouraging march, he entered a city to find someplace to sleep. He was turned out of several inns because he was a foreigner. Then the police began to shadow him, and he didn't know where to turn.

Finally, a young man offered to help him. They trudged around the city without success until one o'clock in the morning, and then the young man abandoned him. He had to spend the rest of the night on the steps of a temple with three thieves lurking in the shadows, waiting for him to fall asleep so they could murder him and take his effects. Taylor stayed awake the rest of the night, singing songs and repeating Bible verses to himself until the thieves gave up in disgust and left. Only then did he manage to catch a few moments' sleep.

In the morning the young man who had taken him
through the streets came back and demanded an out-
rageous fee for his "guide service." This was too
much. Hudson Taylor lost his temper, grabbed the
fellow by the arm, shook him, and told him to shut
up and go away. Weary, broken, and dispirited, he
started the long, painful journey back to Shanghai.
For eight long miles he dragged himself along in
spiritual rebellion, wondering why God had abandoned him in this way.

Then, suddenly, he realized that he had, in effect,
denied his Lord. All his anger and pain melted into
tears of repentance as the truth broke through to him
that he had never asked God's guidance and protection along the way. He had been so intent upon his
own trouble that he had forgotten to commit the
matter to the Lord.

He relates in his journal that as he went along he
confessed the whole thing and asked the Lord to forgive him. And at that moment there came flooding
into his heart a glorious sense of the presence and forgiveness of Christ. The initiative and control passed
once again from Hudson Taylor to the Lord where it
belonged.

This was what God wanted. When Dr. Taylor got
to Shanghai, he found a letter waiting for him with a
check in it for the exact amount to cover his loss. And
he learned soon that if he had gone on to Swatow, he
would have arrived just in time to be imprisoned, and
perhaps executed. All the fretful worry, gnawing
fear, the despair, and the perplexity that he experienced was totally unnecessary. The *events* might have
been the same, regardless of whether he prayed or
not, but the *emotions* he experienced would have been
far different if he had only prayed, "Lord, lead me not
into temptation."

All three of the requests in the Lord's Prayer reflect the one great truth that Jesus labors to impress upon us: we are forever in need—body, soul, and spirit. Only as we walk step by step in continual dependence upon a living God can any of this need ever be adequately met. When we fail to pray this simple, child-like prayer out of our hearts, expressing it in whatever words we choose, we are simply exposing ourselves to unnecessary disturbance, upset, and failure.

Our Father, we can only echo these words our Lord Jesus taught us. Give us this day our daily bread, forgive us our sins, lead us not into temptation. In Christ's name, Amen.

PART II

Asking, seeking, or knocking—the answer is certain, if we believe God. Faith takes his answer for granted. All fulfillment of need is an activity of the Holy Spirit, but, mysteriously, he waits until we ask before he moves. The invisible events of heaven, which will be reflected on earth, are determined in the heart of a praying Christian. Because Jesus went to the Father, he will now, through us, do greater works—of permanent value—than he was able to do while on earth. A Christian's work is never anything but borrowed activity, based on borrowed authority, empowered by borrowed deity.

And he said to them, "Which of you who has a friend will go to him at midnight and say to him, 'Friend, lend me three loaves; for a friend of mine has arrived on a journey, and I have nothing to set before him'; and he will answer from within, 'Do not bother me; the door is now shut, and my children are with me in bed; I cannot get up and give you anything'? I tell you, though he will not get up and give him anything because he is his friend, yet because of his importunity he will rise and give him whatever he needs. And I tell you, Ask, and it will be given you; seek, and you will find; knock, and it will be opened to you. For every one who asks receives, and he who seeks finds, and to him who knocks it will be opened. What father among you, if his son asks for a fish, will instead of a fish give him a serpent; or if he asks for an egg, will give him a scorpion? If you then, who are evil, know how to give good gifts to your children, how much more will the heavenly Father give the Holy Spirit to those who ask him!" (Luke 11:5-13).

6
PRAYER'S CERTAINTIES

Immediately following our Lord's model prayer, which he intended for us to use as a guide, he continues his response to his disciples' urgent cry, "Lord, teach us to pray," by telling the familiar parable of the importunate friend. Let us see what Jesus wants us to learn from this parable; here is the introduction:

> *And he said to them, "Which of you who has a friend will go to him at midnight and say to him, 'Friend, lend me three loaves; for a friend of mine has arrived on a journey, and I have nothing to set before him'; and he will answer from within, 'Do not bother me; the door is now shut, and my*

*children are with me in bed; I cannot get up and
give you anything'?" (Luke 11:5-7).*

The link with prayer in this story is very evident.
True prayer never occurs apart from a sense of need,
and the first note in the story Jesus tells is one of dire,
pressing *necessity*. Here is a friend who comes after
midnight and announces that another friend has arrived on a journey unexpectedly, and he simply has
nothing in the house to give him.

Nothing to Offer

Often others' needs seem more demanding to us
than our own. I rather suspect that this man would
never have gone over to his friend's house in the
middle of the night to borrow bread to meet his own
hunger. But when a friend arrives after a long journey
and is hungry, a deep sense of necessity makes him
willing to go to his neighbor to ask for bread even
though it is late and he knows his neighbor is in bed.

It has been suggested that there is a note of audac-
ity here. As someone has said, "He may not have any
bread, but he certainly has plenty of crust, going
after midnight and waking this fellow up out of a
sound sleep!" But it is obvious, as our Lord tells the
story with this touch of humor in it (and I think it
was intentional) that this man is driven by a deep
sense of concern. He simply has nothing to give his
hungry friend and is forced to go to his neighbor for
help.

Is there anything quite so likely to bring us to our
knees in prayer as the request of another person for
our help, and the shattering awareness that we
simply *have nothing to give?*

One evening recently my telephone rang at ten
o'clock. I picked it up and recognized the voice of a
relatively new Christian, a young man who has been

growing wonderfully in Christian love and grace. There was a note of desperation in his voice as he told me that his wife had just phoned to tell him that she was bringing a friend home to talk with him. His wife is not yet a Christian. In fact, she has been somewhat resistant to the gospel and has given him a good deal of difficulty since he became a Christian.

It seems that she had run across an old school friend, an unmarried schoolteacher, who was utterly lonely and desperate and was threatening suicide. Even though the wife was not yet a believer, she knew that there was something in the Christian message that could help the unfortunate and the despairing, and she was bringing her friend over to talk to her husband. In the meantime he was calling me to ask, "What shall I tell her?"

Perhaps you well know that strange, sinking sensation when someone asks for help and you do not know what to say. Immediately there is a sense of pressure, almost terror. *"What shall I say?"* Perhaps a neighbor comes for coffee and suddenly a question arises or a problem is laid bare; perhaps a school friend stammers out a question as you are walking to school, or a letter arrives from a friend or relative with an urgent plea. Or possibly a friend invites you out to lunch and over the dessert pours out a pitiful tale, or your child brings home a problem from school and stands expectantly, waiting for an answer, and you ask yourself, "What can I say?" The best you can do is stall and hope for a quiet moment when you can rush to your Great Neighbor and cry out to him, "A friend has come, and I have nothing to set before him." This happens often, doesn't it? But it is out of such moments of deep necessity that true prayer is born.

Then our Lord moves on immediately to sound a note of absolute and profound *certainty.*

> *"I tell you, though he will not get up and give him*
> *anything because he is his friend, yet because of his*
> *importunity he will rise and give him whatever he*
> *needs. And I tell you, Ask, and it will be given*
> *you; seek, and you will find; knock, and it will be*
> *opened to you. For every one who asks receives, and*
> *he who seeks finds, and to him who knocks it will be*
> *opened" (Luke 11:8-10).*

That is an amazing declaration. There are staggering implications here. Some interpret verse eight as
though our Lord is saying that we must belabor God
with our prayers, as if the only way we can expect to
get anything from God is to be importunate, to per-
sist in prayer, to hound him until he gives in and
gives us our request.

God Is Not Reluctant

But I am absolutely sure that Jesus is teaching
quite the opposite. Both in the parable of the importunate widow and in this parable of the importunate
friend he is simply using a vivid contrast to set before
us the truth he wants us to learn. In fact, he goes on to
say, clearly, unmistakably, that God is *not* like that
sleepy, reluctant neighbor who doesn't want to get
up out of bed.

Sometimes we ascribe the reason for our failure in
prayer to the supposition that we have not been persistent enough. We find prayer irksome, difficult,
and unpleasant, and we simply say, "I know I should
pray more; I know if I did, more things would happen," for we are obsessed with this idea that God is a
reluctant God who must be wheedled out of things.

But Jesus says this is not the case. The only possible meaning that we can give to verses nine and ten
is that God gives willingly, freely, without fail, to
every child who comes to him. "Ask, and it shall be

given; seek, and you shall find; knock, and it shall be opened." And verses eleven and twelve can only mean that he does not tantalize us by holding out false hopes in prayer: "What father among you, if his son asks for a fish, will instead of a fish give him a serpent; or if he asks for an egg, will give him a scorpion?" He is saying that God does not give capriciously or vindictively; he means what he says. You, as an earthly father, would not give in such a manner—neither does God.

Take careful note of what he does say, for he suggests that there are three levels of prayer: ask, seek, and knock. (You can remember them, incidentally, if you will notice that the initial letters of each word spell "ask": "a" ask, "s" seek, "k" knock.) Now mark these three different levels. The circumstances of each are vastly different, but the answer is always the same. That is what Jesus is saying.

Ask in Faith

The simplest and easiest level, of course, is *ask*. What Jesus means is that there are certain needs which require a mere asking to be immediately and invariably met, and the range of these needs is far wider than we usually give God credit for. For instance, in reading through the New Testament it becomes clear that our need for Christlike attitudes lies in this category. If we need love, courage, wisdom, power, patience—they all lie in this realm. Simply ask, that is all. Ask, and immediately the answer is given.

Isn't that what James says, "If any of you lacks wisdom . . ." What? "Let him ask God who gives to all men generously and without reproaching," and then what? "It will be given him" (James 1:5). That's all, it shall be given.

But someone protests, "I have tried this. Not long ago I was in a situation in which I felt I did not know the answer, so I shot up a prayer, 'Lord, help me, give me wisdom,' and nothing happened. I went on to say the most inane and foolish things. It doesn't work." Now, stop a minute. Is God a liar? Does he say he will give and then fail to do so? Is he like a father, a wicked, cruel, and vicious father who gives us a scorpion when we ask for an egg, or gives us a snake when we ask for a fish? No, the question is not did he give, but did you receive? Did you ask *in faith,* did you believe God when you asked? Did you take? Remember that James goes on to say:

> *But let him ask in faith, with no doubting, for he who doubts is like a wave of the sea that is driven and tossed by the wind. For that person must not suppose that a double-minded man, unstable in all his ways, will receive anything from the Lord (James 1:6-8).*

All God's gifts are given to faith, not to unbelief. The problem here is: What do you do after you have asked? What were you expecting when you asked God for wisdom? How did you think he would give it? Were you waiting for a sense of wisdom, some kind of clarifying of the brain or increased mental power so that you could see all the answers clearly? Were you expecting a feeling of power, some tingling stream that ran down your backbone and out to the ends of your nerves? Is this what you were waiting for?

No, faith takes the answer for granted. God is faithful, God gives, and when we ask, we must take it for granted that he has given. Then, whatever word comes to our lips, we must count on the fact that it is the very word of wisdom or the word of power or the word of patience that we need. God loves to be trusted, but only faith can lay hold of what he gives, and when faith is there, the need is invariably met.

When Jesus says, "Ask, and it shall be given," he does not say the answer will be accompanied by any feelings or signs or emotions. Just take it for granted, thank God, step out on it—the answer is there.

Listen and Look

A second level of prayer is denoted by this word "seek." You cannot think of what it means to seek without understanding that our Lord indicates that an element of time is involved. Seeking is not a single act. It is a process, a series of acts.

Every mother knows that husbands and children think of seeking as a single act. They will stand in the middle of a room and cast one sweeping glance around it, looking for a lost object, and then call for help. "Mom, where is so-and-so?" And mother opens the drawer or moves the bottle or lifts the paper and there it is. I am convinced that my wife is a master of sleight-of-hand, for I cannot understand how, when she looks for it, an object will suddenly appear right in the place I had just looked without finding it.

Searching involves a process. Jesus says there are areas of life that require more than asking: there must be seeking, searching. Something is lost, hidden from us, and prayer then becomes a search, a plea for insight, for understanding, for an unraveling of the mystery with which we are confronted. Again, the answer is absolutely certain. Seek, and you *will* find!

God's Purpose Revealed

We have an example of this truth in that well-known incident in the life of the Apostle Paul, when he was suffering from that painful affliction he called "a thorn in the flesh." It was obviously a physical disability which hounded and limited him—at least he felt it did. Three times he asked to have this taken away, but there was no answer. So the Apostle realized that this was not the kind of thing that is removed by asking; it requires a search. As he meditated and searched out this thing, waiting upon God, the answer came to him, "My grace is sufficient for you" (2 Corinthians 12:9). In other words, "It is better this way, Paul. I have allowed this deliberately to come into your life, and I will not remove it, for my grace is sufficient for you. I can give you all that it takes to stand this thing, for what it is doing for you is of far more value than anything that would come by its removal." So Paul says, "I have learned, therefore, to glory in my infirmities, my weaknesses, because then the power of Christ rests upon me."

Now what had prayer done? Prayer had broken through the mysterious barrier, the seeming wall of silence, that met the Apostle when he asked to have this thing removed. As he prayed about it, his mind was illuminated. He began to see that behind his disability, God's purposes were at work, and they were of such tremendous value that he cried, "Gladly, Lord, will I endure the physical infirmity that the great and abiding values of this suffering may not be lost upon me in Jesus Christ."

So, the searching prayer was answered. We need not go on in confusion and uncertainty in these perplexing areas of life where the final solution is long delayed. In such instances the answer is found in seeking. Seek, and ye shall find. The answer is absolutely certain.

For Closed Doors

There is still a third level of prayer which involves knocking. Here, both time and repetition are involved. Knocking is not a single rap; it is a series of raps. It is a request for admittance, repeated if necessary, and it suggests situations where we seek an entrance or an opportunity. Someone has perhaps erected a barrier against our witness or against our friendship and we are seeking to surmount that, to get behind the wall of resistance, and to have an opportunity freely and openly to speak to or to share in or to enter into a life. That requires knocking.

Perhaps we have an unshakeable desire to begin a certain type of work or ministry from which we are now excluded. We long to move into that area, and we feel God is leading us, calling us, to be this or to do that. That requires knocking. We hunger, perhaps, after knowledge or friendship or as the Word of God says, "hungering and thirsting after righteousness." We are looking for an opportunity, seeking an entrance into an area that is now restricted from us. This requires knocking. We come before God and boldly and repeatedly ask, each time making an endeavor to enter the door of opportunity, for we are resting on the solid assurance that what Jesus says here is true, "Knock, and it shall be opened."

There is a remarkable and clear-cut example of this in Paul's letter to the Romans. As he writes to these dear friends, many of whom he had never met but knew by reputation only, he says,

> *For God is my witness, whom I serve with my spirit in the gospel of his Son, that without ceasing I mention you always in my prayers {Without ceasing! As he prays that this door might be opened to him, he knocks without ceasing.}, asking that somehow by God's will I may now at last succeed in coming to you. For I long to see you, that I may impart to you some spiritual gift to strengthen you, that is, that we may be mutually encouraged by*

each other's faith, both yours and mine (Romans 1:9-12).

Here is an area that he wished to enter, but he was frustrated again and again. But he kept trying, knowing that to him who knocks, it shall be opened. And the book of Acts tells us that he did finally reach Rome one day, a prisoner in chains. God brought him to Rome, and from his prison cell in Rome there came his "Prison Epistles," the greatest letters the Apostle ever wrote.

Prayer is not simply asking; prayer is also seeking and knocking; but the answer is invariably the same, for everyone who asks receives, and he who seeks finds, and to him who knocks it will be opened.

To Him Who Believes

Now if prayer begins with necessity and moves on to certainty, then assuredly it ends on a note of ability: "If you then, who are evil, know how to give good gifts to your children, how much more will the heavenly Father give the Holy Spirit to those who ask him!" (Luke 11:13).

This is one of the greatly misunderstood passages of Scripture, and it is often taken to refer to the initial indwelling of the Holy Spirit in the human heart. Some people have been led by this passage to feel that it is possible to be a Christian and not have the Holy Spirit, and perhaps years after conversion they must ask God for the Spirit to be given to them. But that is not the meaning of the passage at all. Both John and Paul make it clear, explicitly clear, that the Spirit of Christ, the Holy Spirit, is received the moment we believe in Jesus Christ. It is recorded in John's Gospel that Jesus stood at the last day of the feast and cried, "If any one thirst, let him come to me and drink. He who believes in me, as the scripture has said, 'Out of his heart shall flow rivers of living water.'" And John immediately adds, "Now this he said about the Spirit, which *those who believe in him* would receive" (John 7:37-39).

And Paul says that by one Spirit we were all (all believers) baptized into one body, the Body of Christ (1 Corinthians 12:13). The Spirit of God does not come by invitation initially. This word about asking for the Spirit is not addressed to unbelievers, but to believers who already have the Holy Spirit!

This is the paradox of Christianity: Though it is true that all Christians have the indwelling Holy Spirit, it is also true, and we are not speaking nonsense when we say this, that we need continually to be filled with the Holy Spirit. That does not mean the Holy Spirit comes in again and again but that we give ourselves over to his occupancy and his mastery in our lives. All fulfillment of need is then an activity of the Holy Spirit, and this is why Jesus ends this enlightening passage on prayer by reminding us that every Christian is to be continually asking for and receiving that flow of the Spirit's power which alone enables him to do anything in God's sight.

For an illustration of this, I refer to the life of Oswald Chambers, who wrote *My Utmost for His Highest*. Oswald Chambers was a philosophy tutor at Dunoon College in England. He was a genuine Christian, there is no question about it. His faith in Christ as his Savior was sincere and unshakeable. But as he lived on as a Christian, there came to him a very deep conviction that, though he knew he was a Christian, he also knew that he was an appallingly dull, often defeated, sadly disillusioned Christian.

This despair and defeat continued until it reached a climax. The climax came at the time of a visit to the college by Dr. F. B. Meyer, who was mightily used of God in proclaiming the Spirit-filled life. During Dr. Meyer's visit, there was awakened in Oswald Chambers's heart a realization that his life was very barren. He records his feelings at that time: "If this is all there is to Christianity, if I have got all there is, then the thing's a fraud." He became very hungry for something more of God.

On this particular occasion Dr. Meyer preached from this very verse, Luke 11:13, and Oswald Chambers said the truth penetrated his heart with gripping power: "How much more will the heavenly Father give the Holy Spirit to those who ask him!" There was a brief but fierce battle in his thinking, and at last he simply responded to the verse and said, "Lord, all right, I ask you now for the Holy Spirit and I take him. I receive him from you now in faith."

The result was nothing emotional, there was no feeling of power, there was no sense of vision, there was no deeper realization of God—nothing! Oswald Chambers's next step was to talk it all out with a friend, and during the conversation the friend reminded him that Jesus said, "You shall receive power when the Holy Spirit has come upon you" (Acts 1:8). This is simply a gift from the Lord to be taken, to be accepted, that's all.

Like a flash the sudden realization came to Oswald Chambers that in reality he was asking God to give him a sense of power so he could hold it in his hand, as it were, and say, "Look, this is what I got by laying my all on the altar." And he said, "I came to realize that God intended me, having asked, to simply take it by faith, and that power would be there. I might see it only by the backward look but I was to reckon on the fact that God would be with me to do." Five years later he recorded the results:

If the previous four years of my life had been noth-
ing but hell on earth, the last five have been heaven
on earth. Every aching abyss of my heart has been
filled with the overflowing love of God. Love is the
beginning, the middle, and the end.

Now did that mean the Holy Spirit was not present in Oswald Chambers's heart before he had this experience? Of course not. How else was he a Christian?
How else did he realize that Jesus Christ was his, except as the Spirit bore witness with his spirit that he
was a child of God? What happened was that he gave
over the willing consent of his life to the Holy Spirit
to direct his activities, and he accepted the Word of
God as sufficient proof that it would all happen as he
walked on that promise. And this is what the verse
means. It takes power to live a Christian life. You
know that, don't you? It takes power to knock all the
self-conceit and the self-centeredness out of our lives,
and it takes power to keep Christ central in everything. This power does not come by the earnest grit-
ting of our teeth and striving to achieve it. It comes
by a continual asking and taking, by a continual
praying by faith, "Lord, take me, truly take me,
Lord," and then expecting that he has done it. When
we do that, God writes upon us the marks of power
and sends us out as living epistles to be read and
known of all men.

Lord Jesus, in this moment we ask that these words
may come with fresh and vital meaning to our
hearts. Help us to see that there is a vast and great
experience of your blessing and power lying before
us, waiting for us to step out upon the basis of your
word alone. Open our eyes to the realization that
there are things we need to ask for and take

immediately from your hand, other things that we need to seek for, and still others for which we need to knock and wait, and knock again, knowing that in every case without exception your word is sure, your answer is true. It shall be given, we shall find, it shall be opened. In Jesus' name, Amen.

"Truly, I say to you, whatever you bind on earth shall be bound in heaven, and whatever you loose on earth shall be loosed in heaven. Again I say to you, if two of you agree on earth about anything they ask, it will be done for them by my Father in heaven. For where two or three are gathered in my name, there am I in the midst of them" (Matthew 18:18-20).

7
PRAYING
TOGETHER

These words from Matthew 18:18-20 are almost frightening in their implications. They reveal both the most attractive and most fearsome thing about prayer—its authority. Prayer is a powerful thing.

"Prayer has already divided seas and rolled up flowing rivers, it has made flinty rocks gush into fountains, it has quenched flames of fire, it has muzzled lions, disarmed vipers and poisons, it has marshalled the stars against the wicked, it has stopped the course of the moon and arrested the sun in its race, it has burst open iron gates and recalled souls from eternity, it has conquered the strongest devils and commanded legions of angels down from heaven. Prayer has bridled and chained the raging passions of men and destroyed vast armies of proud, daring, blustering atheists. Prayer has brought one man from the bottom of the sea and carried another in a chariot of fire to heaven." That is not mere hyperbole, that is historical fact. Prayer has done a great many other things as well. It is an awesome, mighty force in the world of men.

Something Like Magic

In this passage of Scripture we have three very illuminating insights into prayer from the greatest authority on prayer in all the world. First, we see that prayer is *an authority which operates in mystery:* "Truly, I say to you, whatever you bind on earth shall be bound in heaven, and whatever you loose on earth shall be loosed in heaven" (v. 18). Binding and loosing. As you read these words, it sounds almost like magic, doesn't it? In the fairy tales that we read as children there was always some magic object, a lamp, a ring, or a magic word with which a person could do the strangest things. He could turn people into toads; he could cast spells of enchantment and create instant castles and bridges; he could travel by carpet or even on the wind.

In this one point at least, prayer is indeed somewhat like magic. For what our Lord is unquestionably saying here is that it is possible for quite ordinary humans like you and me to exercise extraordinary power, and that heaven will in some sense ratify what is done on earth. He is saying that we will be put in touch with a world beyond the commonplace world which is visible to our senses.

This is certainly what he means by the contrast between heaven and earth in this verse. Surely we must take these words seriously. We realize that it does not mean that prayer is magic or that we can do whatever we fancy—acting by caprice and changing people into all kinds of strange objects. There are limitations to prayer, and these we will observe as we go along. But I think we must understand first what Jesus means when he speaks of heaven and earth. What is heaven? Where is heaven?

To ask *where* is to reveal a basic misunderstanding of heaven, for too often we think of it in terms of space: earth is "down here"; heaven is "up there" somewhere. The Russians once made a great deal of this concept. They said they launched their cosmonauts into space and looked for heaven, but could not find it. There was no sign of it "up there," and so they came to the conclusion that it simply did not exist.

How pitiful, we say, that men should be so ignorant as to think they could see heaven in terms of physical things! And yet, I am afraid we reveal the same weakness in our own thinking about heaven, for this verse is taken often to mean that down here on earth we are given certain powers to bind or loose, and God up in heaven is forced to ratify our actions and fulfill them. On this concept is based the Catholic doctrine of forgiveness. They say the Church is empowered by this verse to forgive sins, and when the priest says, "Absolvo te" (your sins are forgiven), God in heaven must forgive sins on the basis of this verse.

This is all the unfortunate result of faulty thinking about heaven. Heaven is not spatially determined. It is not up there while we are down here, nor is it to be thought of in terms of time. We think of earth as now, this life. Heaven, then, is later—after death. But I do not think the Scripture uses the word in that sense.

It is true that heaven exists after life, but what our
Lord Jesus is saying here is that heaven exists at the
same time as earth—both are a part of this life. This
is more than saying that the decisions which we must
make in this life produce ultimate results in heaven
after death, although it is certainly true. But Jesus is
saying simply that heaven is the silent, invisible,
spiritual kingdom which lies all about us, encom-
passing us, enclosing us, embracing us, waiting for
us to recognize it. Entering the kingdom of heaven
means we *recognize* that kingdom, we believe in it, we
act upon its reality. In the Beatitudes, Jesus gave us
the clue to entering: "Blessed are the poor in spirit,
for theirs is the kingdom of heaven" (Matthew 5:3).

Reflections of Heaven

Earth, as opposite to heaven, is the world of sense
which demands our attention day and night throughout all of life. That which we touch and feel and see
and sense through our five senses is earth. But heaven
is not merely future; heaven is also present, and
equally as real as earth. It parallels our familiar physical world, Jesus is saying, and the doors between
these two worlds are open.

This verse says there is a correspondence between
heaven and earth. The outer world of time and space
and events and history with which we are so familiar
is but a reflection of that inner world, that invisible
world which lies all about us, which is God's spiritual
kingdom. In other words, earth is in some sense a reflection of heaven.

With our physical senses we cannot see that inner
world. All we see is its reflection in the outer world of
history. It is somewhat like the back of your head,
which you have never seen. All you can see, at best, is
but a reflection of it in a mirror. Then you see the

back of your head, not in actuality, but in reflection. You see only the image of it.

In the Christian philosophy of history, the events which are reported in our daily newspapers are simply reflections of what has taken place in the invisible world of spirit—heaven, if you like—which is within us and around us. And the amazing thing which Jesus says here is that the invisible things which take place in heaven and will be reflected on earth are determined, not in heaven, but on earth in the heart of a praying Christian. Whatever we bind in this outward, conscious life of ours, in touch with the things of sense, will be confirmed in that invisible world and will find its reflection again on earth in the things of this life.

Admittedly there is mystery here. I do not think any of us can understand exactly why it is that God waits till Christians pray before he begins to do what he has intended all along and even announced that he will do, but it is an indisputable fact that that is exactly what he does. He waits till someone prays before he moves.

We read that when Daniel was an old man, he read in the account of Jeremiah that the Babylonian captivity was about to reach its close, having run the predicted course of seventy years. Daniel was moved to pray mightily that God would send the captives of Israel back to their homeland. But those captives did not begin to return until Daniel prayed! The principle is also recorded for us in James 4:2, "You do not have, because you do not ask." It is that simple. God waits until we ask before he moves.

In our United States government there are certain powers which we could call powers of binding and loosing that are granted to the president and to him alone. Only the president, for instance, can sign treaties with foreign powers and thus bind this nation to another. There is no other individual in our government who is authorized to affix his signature to a treaty and to cause it to take effect.

Only the president can loose the atomic might of this nation. So important is this matter of deciding when to send our great missiles screaming into space that the power to do so has been delegated to one man only, the president of the United States. Further, only the president can pardon certain criminals and loose them from the penalty which the law demands. The whole nation might, under certain circumstances, desire the president to act in a certain way and might exert tremendous moral force upon him to act, but until he takes action, there is nothing that can be done.

Absolute Power

Jesus is telling us in Matthew 18:18 that God has granted powers of binding and loosing to every believer, and until we act upon them, nothing happens. In the realm of our personal lives these powers are almost absolute. God has said that we have power to bind every form of evil in our own lives. There is nothing that needs to have dominion over us. In Romans 6:14 Paul wrote, "For sin will have no dominion over you, since you are not under law but under grace." By grace we have power to bind every evil force, every contrary authority within us. Paul also tells us that our warfare is not against flesh and blood but is along spiritual lines (2 Corinthians 10:3-4). We are warring against evil authorities and powers in high places, and we have power to bring them under control in our own lives as we reckon ourselves dead to sin and alive to God.

Furthermore, we have power to loose the full flood of the Spirit's resources in our own lives. There is not one of us that has any excuse for not being all that God intends us to be. Someone has well said that *we are as victorious as we want to be.* No matter what you have been, no matter how weak, how failing, how faltering, you have been exactly as victorious as you have wanted to be. Power has been granted to us in Jesus Christ to bind every contrary force, every evil motive in our lives, and to loose the flood of the Spirit's power through us—not only in our own lives, but in others as well.

This is the meaning of intercessory prayer. Others can be helped tremendously by our prayers. I have often seen young people, in their early Christian experience, drift into a condition of apathy and indifference. They become unconcerned about spiritual values, gradually slipping into coarseness, wrong habits, degenerating moral principles—and then, suddenly, they begin to change, almost overnight. Their attitude shifts 180° from what it was before. They begin to take an interest in spiritual matters again and to grow spiritually. A new light comes into their eyes; they are totally different. What happened? Sooner or later it is discovered that someone has become concerned and was praying for that young couple. No one may have been at all aware of what was happening, but prayer was changing a life.

As we look at the words in the Scripture text about binding and loosing, we can see that although we do not understand all about them, it is apparent that prayer is authority—an authority which operates in mystery. It is the link to that invisible world which is the control center of all human life. We stand on the frontier between two worlds when we pray.

Therefore, as James says, "The prayer of a righteous man has great power in its effects" (James 5:16).

Amazing Arithmetic

Prayer is not only an authority that works in mystery, but it is also *an authority which is expressed in unity:* "Again I say to you, if two of you agree on earth about anything they ask, it will be done for them by my Father in heaven" (Matthew 18:19).

This is the charter for the prayer meeting. One Christian praying alone has great effect, but what happens when two or more gather together? It is evident here that there is an amazing arithmetic about prayer. In Deuteronomy, Moses told the people of Israel, "One of you shall chase a thousand, but two of you shall chase ten thousand." That is a strange ratio, isn't it? If it were straight arithmetic, we would say one should chase a thousand, two should chase two thousand. But when two Christians get together there is a geometric increase in the effect of their prayers. Two shall put ten thousand to flight.

From the earliest days the Church has felt the need to gather together in prayer. In the fourth chapter of Acts we see the Church gathered for prayer after they had been persecuted by the Sanhedrin. There is another account in Acts 12 when the Church met and prayed for Peter, and he was delivered from prison. They could hardly believe it, but it was true. This is corporate prayer. What is the purpose of prayer like this? Jesus says it is that we might agree together. "If two of you agree on earth about anything they ask, it will be done for them by my Father in heaven."

Words are fascinating things; there are at least eight words in the Greek New Testament that are translated "agree." One of them means literally "to stand together." It means two people make a common decision. This is the way many people understand this verse. It is taken to mean that if a person wants something, he finds someone else who wants the same thing. Then they agree on it in prayer, and God must honor their prayer and do their will.

But that is not what this means at all. "Agree," as it is used here, means "to sound together, to harmonize." Two related notes struck on the piano will harmonize. But the harmony is already there, it is simply brought out as you strike the right notes.

This verse pictures two Christians coming together in this way: One says what is on his heart, what he believes God wants him to pray for, and the other says what is on *his* heart, what *he* believes God wants him to pray for. Where they find they agree, where they harmonize, where they sound together, those are the areas where they can fully expect God to work—God says, "It shall be done." There is a glorious definiteness about that, isn't there? It shall be done!

This is why I like to hear people say "Amen" at prayer meetings. I am old fashioned enough to enjoy hearing a good "Amen" now and then, and after all, it is exactly what the Scriptures suggest. When one person is leading in prayer, everyone else is listening, or ought to be, and when something is said which strikes a responsive chord, they say "Amen," either silently or vocally. What they are really saying is, "I agree; this is what God has said to me, too." When there are amens sprinkled throughout a prayer meeting, either vocally or silently, it marks the areas of firm agreement where the Spirit of God is at work bringing unity. This is where prayer finds its authority.

The board of elders in our church has long since learned that the mind of the Spirit is determined

when all fourteen men meeting together are brought
into a sense of unity. When they feel there is unity,
they feel God's will has been discovered. This is what
Jesus is saying, "Where two or three of you sound the
same note, not by comparing notes beforehand, but
simply, voluntarily, spontaneously, it shall be done
by my Father in heaven."

Further, it is evident in verse twenty that prayer is
also *an authority which originates in personality:* "For
where two or three are gathered in my name, there
am I in the midst of them." Don't miss the force of
that little introductory word, "for." *"For,* where two
or three are gathered together in my name." Here is
the explanation of the mystery in verse eighteen. I
confess that I do not fully understand how it is that a
man or woman or boy or girl, praying on the basis of
the binding and loosing powers granted by God, can
move such mighty forces that prayer frequently en-
gages. But of course, it is not merely a man praying,
but *Christ* is in him and *He* is praying. It is Christ
praying through him. "For God is at work in you,"
Paul says, "both to will and to work for his good
pleasure" (Philippians 2:13).

Now you can see how clearly this reveals that
Christians are creatures of two worlds. In our humanity, like everyone else of the human race, we belong
to earth. We live in a world of space and time, touching the events around us and reacting to them as
others do. We read the same newspapers, hear the
same television reports, and are subject to the same
pressures as the world about us. We are creatures of
earth.

But in the new life in Jesus Christ, in the heaven-
lies where we live in Christ, we are creatures of
heaven and are in touch with the invisible world—
the world which controls the outer world. We are

standing, as I said, on the frontier between those two worlds. As someone has well put it, prayer, therefore, is God the Son praying to God the Father in the power of God the Spirit, and the prayer room is the believer's heart. That is the whole story of prayer.

With All Saints

Now this indwelling personality is not only the explanation of the mystery of the power of prayer, but it is also the source of the unity we have talked about. In writing to the Ephesians, Paul said that Jesus Christ is "far above all rule and authority and power and dominion, and above every name that is named, not only in this age but also in that which is to come; and he has put all things under his feet and has made him the head over all things for the church, which is his body, the fulness of him who fills all in all" (Ephesians 1:21-23). In other words, the expression of the power of Jesus Christ is never fully seen in an individual Christian, but only in the Church as a whole. The simplest form of the Church is here described, "Where two or three are gathered together in my name."

You and I as individual Christians cannot fully reflect Jesus Christ. It is only when two or three—or two or three hundred or two or three thousand—are gathered together in his name that in a full and complete sense all the power which is committed to Jesus Christ is fully manifested in this life. This means we can never fully know Jesus Christ unless we know him in relation to someone else.

In Ephesians 3:18-19 Paul prays that we may know what is the breadth and length and depth and height, and come to know *with all saints* the love which is in Christ Jesus. "With all saints." We will never know it by ourselves. We can take our Bible

and study it by ourselves, we can analyze it and satu-
rate our minds with it and memorize it, but until we
begin to share it with other Christians, we can never
grasp who Jesus Christ fully is. Furthermore, we can
never learn how mighty and glorious he is unless we
begin to make demands upon his inexhaustible
power and his glory.

"Where two or three are gathered together in my
name," Jesus says, "I am in the midst of them." The
power of the Church does not lie in the numbers that
it can gather together. Many seem to believe that if
we can just get enough people together to pray we
shall have enough power to correct the things that are
wrong in the world and set them right again. Nothing could be further from the truth.

Another misconception is that the power of the
Church is determined by its status in a community.
We seem to think that if we can draw men into the
Church who are in positions of authority or leadership or stature in the community, we will have
enough status to wield great power in the minds and
hearts of men.

How foolish we are. The power of the Church does
not rest in its numbers, its status, its wealth, its
money, its position. The power of the Church of
Jesus Christ is stated right here, "Where two or three
are gathered together in my name, there *I am* in the
midst of them." Out of him alone flows this marvelous power to bind and to loose, and from him alone
comes this tremendous unity by which the mind of
the Spirit becomes known and God can then move
through Christian lives to alter the course and destiny
of the world around us. Let us glory in that! If we
wish to glory in anything, as the early Church did, let
us glory in the fact that Jesus Christ lives and moves
in our midst—that we belong to him, and that his

life is expressed through us. It is only through him that prayer makes its greatest, permanent impact. It is only through his presence that prayer has meaning and value.

Father, what a mistake we make when we try to make things complex. How wonderful it is to come back to simplicity which is in Jesus Christ. How foolish we are to seek substitutes for that simplicity, that simple relationship of a mighty, victorious Lord in the midst of his Church. Lord, teach us to glory in this, teach us to reckon upon it, teach us to pray on this basis and this alone. And, having recognized that these things are true, regardless of what the circumstances around us may be, grant us the faith to step out upon them and act upon them. In Christ's name, Amen.

"Truly, truly, I say to you, he who believes in me will also do the works that I do; and greater works than these will he do, because I go to the Father. Whatever you ask in my name, I will do it, that the Father may be glorified in the Son; if you ask anything in my name, I will do it. If you love me, you will keep my commandments. And I will pray the Father, and he will give you another Counselor, to be with you for ever, even the Spirit of truth, whom the world cannot receive, because it neither sees him nor knows him; you know him, for he dwells with you, and will be in you. I will not leave you desolate; I will come to you" (John 14:12-18).

8
THE HOLY SPIRIT
AND PRAYER

It is significant to note that though Jesus never taught his disciples how to preach, he did teach them how to pray. Much of his teaching on prayer is found in the rich and fragrant passage in the Gospel of John that is called "The Upper Room Discourse." This passage is filled with astonishing concepts; it is one of the most challenging parts of the Word of God. A vast area of mystery and beauty and glory is found in these verses.

Perhaps in this passage, more fully than anywhere else, our Lord unfolds the unique secret of Christianity, that aspect of life which has been called "the exchanged life." This is the secret of a Christian: He is not living his own life; he is living Another's life. Or, more accurately, Another is living his life in him. Until you have grasped that as the mystery and key of Christian living, you have not graduated from the kindergarten level of the Christian life.

It is time now in our study to relate the subject of prayer to the total spectrum of Christian living. There is no passage that does it more effectively than this one in the fourteenth chapter of John. In verses twelve through seventeen, three revelations are given of the life of Jesus Christ at work within us. In verse twelve we learn that the character of a Christian's work is "borrowed activity." In verses thirteen and fourteen we find that the basis of a Christian's prayer is "borrowed authority"; and in verses fifteen through seventeen it is revealed that the secret of a Christian's life is "borrowed deity." This is the actuality of an exchanged life. Let's now explore each of these in detail.

Road to Fulfillment

Each of these divisions consists of a staggering promise of tremendous potential, but we must see that each promise is linked with a limiting or qualifying condition. Frequently as we read these great passages of the Scripture, we are either so dazzled by the promise that we fail to heed the condition, or we are so frightened by the condition that we pay little heed to the promise. But it is necessary that we take very seriously both aspects of what our Lord has said.

Perhaps our greatest problem is to be so awestricken by these promises that we fail to heed the condition. There is a little sign, seen occasionally in offices, which says, "When all else fails, follow directions." Sometimes when we try to lay hold of a promise of God and it does not appear to work, the reason is that we have not followed the directions related to the promise. Thus, a conditioning statement is always the road to fulfillment.

Now in verse twelve the promise is staggering in its implications. Jesus said, "He who believes in me will also do the works that I do; and greater works than these will he do." Although we might accept what Jesus is saying here on a theoretical basis, we find that, practically speaking, his promise is unbelievable. We refuse to accept it at face value. We feel there must be a catch somewhere. Is Jesus really saying that Christians living today in this twentieth century can do not only the works which he did, but also *greater* works than these? Is that what he is saying?

The promise is so overwhelming that we attempt immediately to soften it. We say to ourselves, "Can this be true of me? After all, I am not Jesus Christ, and, therefore, I cannot be expected to do what he did." But how do you square an excuse like that with a verse like this? For in it Jesus plainly says, "He who believes in me will also do the works that I do; and greater works than these will he do."

Here is where we need to observe very carefully exactly what Jesus is saying. For he is not saying here that a sincere, dedicated Christian of today will actually be able, in his sincerity and his dedicated religious effort, to do what Jesus did in the first century. Jesus is not comparing our labors now with his labors then. He is not saying that dedicated Christian men and women are really going to transcend what he accomplished as the Son of God incarnate among men. What Jesus *is* saying, is that as the risen Christ *he* will do through us greater works than *he* did as the incarnate Christ living among men. Do you see the difference?

Notice what he links with this: "because I go to the Father." What does he mean? Simply that it was his going to the Father which released the full potential of the Godhead for human lives and affairs. While he was here on earth, the fullness of God was available to man only in one human body, the body of Jesus Christ. By the strength and indwelling life of the Father he did all the works that we marvel at as we read the story of his life. But what he is saying now is, that as the risen Christ, ascended to the throne of the Father, he himself will do through us, in terms of our personalities and by the activity of our lives, greater works today than he did in the days of his flesh.

A Total Failure

It is rather startling to realize that the work of the incarnate Christ, that is, Jesus Christ of Nazareth working and walking among men, was, at its end, apparently a total and complete failure. We marvel as we read the story of the beginning of his ministry. He performed astonishing miracles—raising men from the dead; healing the sick; opening the eyes of the blind; delivering men, women, and little children from the oppression of demons; touching with his hand the withered arm of a man and restoring it immediately to full growth and life again.

And we read the tremendous words that came from his lips—the Sermon on the Mount; the parables beside the seashore; the countless mysterious, marvelous, and compelling things that he said. It is no wonder that crowds followed him, hounding him, following him even into retreat, insisting upon his ministry. Indeed, it is not surprising that the news spread like wildfire that a prophet had risen in Israel again. Men left their work and their cities and their ordinary activities of life and went out to hear what he had to say, following him for hours on end. That was the beginning.

But at the end, where were the crowds? They had been diminishing for quite some time: "Many of his disciples drew back and no longer went about with him," John tells us (John 6:66). Already many of the searching things that he had been saying had separated the weak from the strong, and toward the end of his ministry the actual number of disciples had been reduced to a handful. And even these, in the hour of his capture and appearance before Pilate, forsook him and fled. In the time of his need they left him. There was only a tiny band of one man and three or four women that gathered around the foot of the cross. That was all the incarnate Christ had to show for the marvelous ministry in the power of the Spirit which he had manifested among men. A total failure! That is the *value* of the works that he did.

Now do you see what he means when he says "greater works than these will you do, because I go to the Father"? His ministry among men, as a man, was a failure. It did not remain; it had no enduring effects. Those who came, attracted by the things they saw, faded back into the shadows when persecution began to grow. No one stayed with him. But there is a very significant promise given in the midst of this Upper Room Discourse when he says to his disciples, "You did not choose me, but I chose you and appointed you that you should go and bear fruit and that your *fruit should abide*" (John 15:16).

Your fruit should remain. What you do in the power of the Spirit will not fade away. Those whom you win to Christ will abide. Christ's cause will flourish in the earth and spread to the uttermost parts till every nation will hear the word, and out of every tribe and nation of earth will come, at last, fruit that will remain.

This is what Jesus meant when he said, "Greater works than these will you do, because I go to the Father." It is *his* work in us. A Christian's true work is borrowed activity. It is never his own, and when he begins to think it is, he defeats every possibility of success. He sabotages the work of the Holy Spirit.

Continually Believing

There is a condition involved here, however. What is it? "He who believes in me." That is the condition. And without fulfillment of the condition the promise will never work.

Notice that Jesus did not say, "He who is a Christian." And I think for good reason. Many people classify themselves as believers because at some time, possibly months or even years ago, they received Jesus Christ in their hearts as Lord and Savior. That is not the meaning here at all. Jesus is using a verb here in the present tense which means, "He who is continually believing in me." He who is appropriating *by faith* that which I am will do these things.

In the Christian life, faith is always the operative word. Jesus is not saying he who holds the truth, but he who acts upon it is the one who will do these works. God gives power and ability only to faith, and it is only when we learn this that these promises come alive. Although we know these promises must be true because of him who spoke them, we see so little evidence of their truth in our living simply because we are not ready to take God at his word and expect him to do great things. It is through an expectant attitude of faith that the promises are realized.

As the basis of a Christian's work, then, is borrowed activity, so the basis of a Christian's prayer is *borrowed authority:* "Whatever you ask in my name, I will do it, that the Father may be glorified in the Son;

if you ask anything in my name, I will do it" (John 14:13, 14). *Whatever, anything,* I will do it. We sense immediately that this promise is too broad. If we take this as absolutely unlimited, a sort of magical Aladdin's lamp that we can rub and ask for anything in the world, certainly we have missed the true point of this passage.

We sense also, almost instinctively, that conflicts would immediately arise if there were no limits connected with the promise. We can see problems arising. What if a Christian athlete is praying for clear weather and a Christian farmer is praying for rain? Which one wins?

No, this promise cannot be limitless; there is a condition here. Our Lord means exactly what he says, but it is essential that we understand precisely what he means. This is a magnificent promise of vast scope, of tremendous encompassment, but what he says is *"if you ask in my name."* This is the condition.

Authorized Activity

That certainly means a great deal more than a kind of magical formula to tack on to the end of our prayers. There is nothing quite as pagan, or silly, as adding "This we ask in Jesus' name" to our prayers without any understanding of whether or not the prayer is actually being asked in Jesus' name. We do this because (1) it is traditionally acceptable, and (2) we do not understand what *in his name* means. In Christ's name means in his authority, on the basis of his character, in the value of his work. Let me illustrate.

All of us are familiar with the phrase, "In the name of the law." Policemen do their business in the name of the law. Now, let's suppose a policeman is sent into a cheap slum area of the city at three o'clock in the afternoon because of some murderous activity that has been reported. When he arrives at the designated address, he knocks at the door and calls out, "Open in the name of the law." After knocking repeatedly without getting an answer, he draws his gun, kicks down the door, and makes his arrest.

Now, let's shift the scene to later that night, possibly ten o'clock. That same policeman is out in a residential area, only now he's off duty and is staggering drunk. In a belligerent attitude he stumbles up the steps of a house, knocks on the door, and shouts, "Open inna name a the law." The people inside hear the commotion and realize there's a drunk at the door, so they refuse to open up. In a rage the policeman breaks down the door, and when he does, the police are called, he is arrested, and taken to jail.

What's the difference? It is the same action, and exactly the same man. Even the words are the same. But the action in the afternoon was done in the name of the law, while the scene at night was done outside the law. One was authorized activity, the other was unauthorized. That is what Jesus means when he says "in my name."

When we ask in Jesus' name we are to ask within the realm and scope of his work and his character. Whatever he is interested in having done on earth, we, as the instruments of his activity, are involved in accomplishing it. "Whatever you need," he says, "ask for it and it shall be done." Whatever! Anything! If it is a need within this limit, you can ask for it and it shall be done without fail.

Let me illustrate again by referring to a breakfast I attended in Newport Beach, California. I had been asked to bring a message, and as is often the case in a time like that, I felt very inadequate and helpless. Here was a wealthy, affluent area. The meeting was held in lavish surroundings in this resort area where great religious indifference was likely to abound. I knew, too, that scores of men would be present who were not in any way outwardly identified with the Christian faith and many of them would be typically shallow, rootless, unconcerned, modern pagans.

It was a challenging situation—an opportunity to speak in the name of God to men who would otherwise never give an ear—and I felt the tremendous challenge and my own inability. I have learned by long experience and by the word of God to recognize that feelings of inadequacy are a good sign. I welcome them now, because I know they are designed to lead me to ask for the help I need.

So, before the meeting began, I asked God for three things: First, I asked that what I said might be relevant, that my words might come to grips with the situation in which these people found themselves. Second, I asked that my words might be challenging and would awaken these men. And third, I asked that my message might be powerful, that its effect would not diminish, and that it would not be lightly swept aside but penetrate their hearts with power.

What I said that morning was neither clever nor profound. Actually, it was very simple. I merely tried to call attention to the moral revolt that is widespread in the United States today and the fact that it is eating away at our national life and destroying the very foundation of our government—things that you read and are hearing today on every side. I tried to point out something of the moral emptiness of such a way of life, how futile and meaningless and purposeless this kind of life seems to be, and what the Christian answer is.

Immediately after the meeting two Chiefs of Police who were present from the cities of Newport

Beach and Costa Mesa came right up to me, visibly moved, shook my hand, and said, "We know what you are talking about. This is the first time we have ever heard anything that seems to suggest an answer. This is what we desperately need down in this area." And one of the mayors who, before the meeting, had insisted, with some asperity, that he would have absolutely no participation in the meeting, stood up at the end to say that he felt I had sounded out the crying need of that area and he hoped this would be an annual event. He also welcomed our team to come down the next week and hold breakfast meetings throughout that entire area.

What is the explanation of that? "Whatever you need, ask, and it shall be given you," that's the answer. If it lies in the direction of the moving of Christ in the affairs of men today, whatever you need, ask. It will be given. Anything! "If you ask anything *in my name,* I will do it."

Now in the last part of our Scripture passage is revealed the fact that the secret of the Christian's life is *borrowed deity.* Jesus said,

> *If you love me, you will keep my commandments.*
> *And I will pray the Father, and he will give you*
> *another Counselor, to be with you for ever, even the*
> *Spirit of truth, whom the world cannot receive, be-*
> *cause it neither sees him nor knows him; you know*
> *him, for he dwells with you, and will be in you*
> *(John 14:15-17).*

What a staggering promise this is! Our Lord is promising here that the One who will come to make his home in every Christian's heart and life is no one less than God himself! The One who comes is the third Person of the Trinity, who supplies to us the fullness of God. "Filled unto the fullness of God" is

Paul's prayer for us, that in the possession of the Holy Spirit we may understand and realize that the One who comes is God himself indwelling us.

Strength and Truth

The names that Jesus uses in John 14:15-17 suggest the richness of this promise. He said that the Spirit will be "another Counselor." I like the old translation better—"Comforter"—but we should understand it in its original meaning. It comes from the word "fortis," that is, "to make strong"; and "com," which means "with." A Comforter is one who stands with you and makes you strong—one who gives strength. In using this word Jesus is saying first of all that he who comes will be the One who has within him the fullness of power, all the strength that we could possibly need.

Then he is called the Spirit of Truth, and that is a wonderful title. Don't you hunger after truth sometimes? In this bewildering world, this perplexing age in which we live, don't you sometimes almost physically hunger for someone, somewhere, somehow, who can tell you the truth? Well, that is who this One is, the Spirit of Truth, the One who unfolds reality, who exposes error, who tears away the veils, who dissolves the mists that confuse and blind us, who removes the doubts and brings us face to face with things as they really are in life.

I read a wonderful testimony by Dr. Emile Caillet about his discovery of the Bible. At the age of twenty-one he had never even seen a Bible, and it wasn't until years later as a married man that he was finally given one. He began to read it and discovered that this was the answer to his lifelong search for what he called "a book that understands me." As he read, he discovered that this book revealed the One who understood him. The Spirit of Truth, who authored the book, told him the truth about himself.

Note, this privilege is exclusively Christian. Only the Christian can be led by the Spirit of God into the nature of reality, into truth. Jesus said, ". . . even the Spirit of truth, *whom the world cannot receive,* because it neither sees him nor knows him." This is for Christians only. The world will never be able to understand reality! As long as men remain worldlings, they are blinded to the ultimate nature of things. They will never understand them because man is both the specimen to be examined and the examiner, and the error that is in the examiner affects the examination! Man reasons continually in a vicious circle of unbelief that prevents him from discovering ultimate reality.

But when the Spirit of Truth comes, he takes away the veils, he dissolves the mists. Little by little, gradually, we begin to understand who we are, and what we are, and why we are what we are, and why others are what they are, and what this world is and where it is going and what its end is going to be. The Spirit of *Truth.* There is nothing more magnificently Christian than this ability to see truth clearly.

Now we come to the condition, for the brutal fact is that though every true Christian has the Spirit of Truth, thousands of them walk in darkness and understand no more about themselves than the blindest pagan around. Though we have the Spirit available to us, we can be as deluded and as blinded as any worldling living next door. Though we have the potential he does not have, we may not enter into it. We may be Bible-taught, but not necessarily Spirit-taught.

Why not? Because Jesus says, ". . . he dwells *with* you, and will be *in* you," and there is a vital distinction in these words. Now, I know as well as you do that every believer, when he receives Jesus Christ, receives the indwelling Spirit of God; that he is *in* us from the beginning. We do not need later to pray for his coming. He is there right from the start. Historically it was true that these disciples were not to receive the indwelling of the Spirit until the day of Pentecost. He dwelt *with* them before, but he was to be *in* them on the day of Pentecost.

Having said all that, however, one thing is still true—although *positionally* the Spirit of God dwells in you, *experientially* it seems as if he merely dwells *with* you. You are not laying hold of his indwelling life, and *for all practical purposes* he is not in you but only with you.

Ready to Obey

This is the explanation for the prevailing weakness in Christian living. A group of us were wrestling with this problem awhile back, and one of the young men who was with us said a very helpful and insightful thing: "You know, I think I know what it is. I have found in my own life that when I simply give up arguing with the Lord and start obeying him, all things begin to work. In my experience I have discovered it is possible to have God at arms' length, dwelling with me. And when he is out there, nothing works. But when I yield to his sovereign direction in my life and begin to act on what he says, then he is *in* me and things begin to happen." He put his finger right on the point. "In you" means that you are under the control of the Holy Spirit and yielding obedience to his totalitarian sovereignty. It means the total collapse of all your rebellion against him.

"Oh," you say, "I'm not in rebellion against the Spirit of God! Why, I'm a Christian. I don't rebel against him." In response, let me ask you, "What kind of life are you living?" Is it God-centered, or is it self-centered? Are your activities and your desires aimed at pleasing yourself? Then you are in rebellion against the Spirit of God. To have him dwelling in you means the total collapse of all revolt, and you can say, "Lord Jesus, your word is my command, I am ready to obey." It is not our relationship *with* Jesus Christ which counts before the world, it is our resemblance *to* him.

> *Holy Spirit, we ask you to search our own hearts on this day and save us from this damnable perfidy of talking truth and not living it, of echoing orthodoxy but refusing to submit in practical ways, of protecting our lives and refusing to fling them into your cause and to abandon ourselves to your purposes. Lord God, what hypocrites we are! Keep us from this, that we may know the fullness of the glory of these promises fulfilled in our lives in this day and age. We ask this in Jesus' name, Amen.*

PART III

Jesus is facing the shadow of the cross as he prays aloud for his disciples, but there is not one word of fear—only an awareness of anticipated opportunity. The hour has come in which all that he had lived for would begin to be fulfilled. He asks to be restored to the place of glory which he enjoyed with the Father before the world was made. While on earth, he had continually laid aside his own glory, emptying himself in order that God might be glorified. This must also be our prayer, for anything less yields nothing but frustration and defeat. While Jesus prays for the Father to keep us in the life-giving relationship with him, he makes it clear that our part—both the easiest and hardest thing in the world—is simply to believe the truth. We will never go any farther than our faith takes us. But the Father is also aiming beyond us; his ultimate target is the entire world, and we must become part of the process of drawing a struggling, rebellious creation to himself.

When Jesus had spoken these words, he lifted up his eyes to heaven and said, "Father, the hour has come; glorify thy Son that the Son may glorify thee, since thou hast given him power over all flesh, to give eternal life to all whom thou hast given him. And this is eternal life, that they know thee the only true God, and Jesus Christ whom thou hast sent" (John 17:1-3).

9
THE TRUE
LORD'S PRAYER

If a number of Christians were asked to repeat the Lord's Prayer, most would begin, "Our Father which art in heaven," for this is universally called "The Lord's Prayer." Actually, though, it is not the Lord's Prayer at all; it is the disciples' prayer. It is the prayer the Lord gave us to pray. But the true Lord's Prayer is found in the seventeenth chapter of John. It has been called "the holy of holies" of the New Testament, for here, in the shadow of the cross, our Lord gathers with his disciples in the Upper Room and in their presence prays to the Father.

I never read this passage without a sense of awe and reverence, but perhaps therein lies a considerable

danger. If we habitually approach this passage with a
sense of its majesty and beauty, we may miss the message because we are afraid to explore in depth what
our Lord is saying.

But if this has been your experience, as I confess it
has been mine, the very purpose our Lord envisioned
when he prayed this prayer has been defeated. For he
deliberately prayed aloud in the presence of his disciples, wanting them to hear what he said, because
the basic relationship that he expresses in this prayer
between himself and the Father is also the relationship that obtains between Jesus and us. There is a
very real sense in which every believer in Jesus Christ
can pray this prayer; it was designed to teach us how
to pray.

Shadow of the Cross

The first three verses of this prayer (John 17:1-3)
set forth the background out of which the prayer
arises—a background of danger and death. It was uttered just a few moments before Jesus left the Upper
Room and, with his disciples, went down into the
dark valley of the Kidron. And continuing across
onto the slopes of the Mount of Olives, he found his
way in the darkness of night into the Garden of
Gethsemane.

There, withdrawing himself from the disciples for
a brief space, he prayed a second, desperate prayer
which wrung the very blood from his body, falling in
great drops to the ground, as he passed into a time of
mysterious and terrible anguish. To that garden
Judas came with the guards who took Jesus prisoner
and led him to Pilate's judgment hall and to the
cross.

Now he is facing the shadow of the cross when he
prays this prayer in the Upper Room. The disciples

are subdued and terrified. They have sensed that
something is wrong; he has told them that he is leaving, and their hearts are wretched with fear and anxiety. But in his prayer there is not one word of fear.

I have in my library a copy of the prayer that
Martin Luther uttered before he appeared before the
Emperor of the Holy Roman Empire in the city of
Worms to answer the charges against him, for which
his very life was at stake. It is a long, rambling, re-
petitive cry of helpless weakness in which Luther
simply casts himself over and over again upon God
for strength and cries out in fear and anguish. But
this prayer of Jesus is entirely different. Instead of a
cry of weakness or a plea for help, the prayer begins
with a powerful awareness of anticipated opportunity: "When Jesus had spoken these words, he lifted
up his eyes to heaven and said, 'Father, the hour has
come'" (John 17:1).

"The hour has come." With these words Jesus
looks forward with obvious anticipation to a time of
boundless opportunity that lies before him. Surely
these words, "the hour has come," mean a good deal
more than the phrase we employ when we face the
end of life, "My time has come." By that we mean we
have come to the end of our rope, the end of life.

Dr. J. Vernon McGee once told of a man who had
been studying through the doctrine of predestination
and had become so entranced by the idea of God's
sovereign protection of the believer under any and
every circumstance that he said to Dr. McGee, "You
know, sir, I am so convinced that God is keeping me
no matter what I do, that I think I could step right
out into the midst of the busiest traffic at noontime,
and if my time had not come, I would be perfectly
safe." Dr. McGee said, very characteristically,

"Well, if you stand in the middle of traffic at noon-time, brother, your time *has* come."

To use a phrase like "my time has come" is resignation, but what Jesus is speaking of here is realization. This is the hour he has been looking forward to all his life, the hour to which he continually refers throughout the record of the Gospels.

In the beginning of John we have the story of the first miracle in Cana of Galilee when Jesus turned the water into wine. There his mother came to him and said, "Son, they have no wine," and his answer was, "Woman, what have you to do with me? My hour has not yet come" (John 2:4). He meant that even though he would perform what his mother had suggested, it would not have the results she anticipated, for the hour had not yet come, the time had not struck. Again and again he said to the disciples, "My hour is not yet." But now, as he approaches the cross, he lifts his eyes to the heavens and says, "Father, the hour has come." By this he means the hour in which all that he had lived for would begin to be fulfilled.

A Grain of Wheat

This anticipation was based upon the principle, as he put it, "Unless a grain of wheat falls into the earth and dies, it remains alone; but if it dies, it bears much fruit" (John 12:24). This is why his hour had not come before: Jesus knew that God's work is never accomplished apart from the principle of death. All the mighty miracles he did and the mighty words he spoke—all the marvelous power of his ministry among men—would be totally ineffective until he had passed through the experience of giving up all that he was. Until that was accomplished, nothing lasting would remain.

Beyond the cross, Jesus knew, lay the glory of God. In Hebrews we read that he endured the cross, despising the shame of it, knowing that beyond it lay the joy which he was awaiting. Beyond the cross lies glory, but the only way to it is through the cross. All of his ministry, all of his life, would be ineffective until he had fulfilled this principle of death. Unless a grain of wheat dies it abides alone; it will never do anything else. It cannot! Only if it dies does it bring forth fruit. Beyond the surrender of his rights lay the possession of privilege; beyond the obedient act was the realized blessing.

This is why we also must pray this prayer, for we are always coming to hours like this in our lives. In both minor and major ways we come to the place where we must say, "Father, the hour has come—the hour where I must make a choice as to whether I shall hold my life for myself, to act in self-centeredness as I have been doing all along, or whether I shall fling it away and, passing into what is apparent death, lay hold of the hope and the glory and the realization that lies beyond it."

Such hours frequently come to all of us. We call them disappointments, setbacks, tragedies, perhaps. We think of them as invasions of our privacy, our right to live our own lives. But if we see them as Jesus saw them, we will recognize that each moment like this is an hour of great possibility which, if we will act on the principle of giving ourselves away, we shall discover an open door to an almost unimaginable realm of service and blessing and glory. That is what Jesus means when he says "The hour is come." It was a time of abounding opportunity.

Power Over All Flesh

Then our Lord continues his prayer: ". . . glorify thy Son that the Son may glorify thee, since thou hast given him power over all flesh, to give eternal life to all whom thou hast given him" (John 17:1-2).

Here is the revelation that he is aware of an adequate relationship. If you look at that verse very carefully, you will notice a marvelous interplay of personality. The Father gives to the Son in order that the Son may give back to the Father. It is not a once-for-all giving in which the Father once gave the Son power over all flesh, but it is a continuous giving. The Father, he says, is continually giving power over all flesh to the Son.

Why? In order that the Son may continually give back to the Father the men whom the Father gives to him that they may be his. And what he is expressing here in this marvelous language is simply that his entire ministry is a manifestation of adequate power for any demand.

The Father gave Jesus power. What for? In order, Jesus says, to give eternal life to whomever the Father has given him—in order to meet the need of any who come to him. Those who are sent of the Father, drawn of the Father, shall come to Jesus. Whoever it may be, the Father has given Jesus everything that is necessary to meet the needs of that person. The Son is equal to any problem, whatever it may be.

During that same week of the prayer breakfast in Newport Beach that I referred to in an earlier chapter, I was in a social gathering in a beautiful home when a man came up to me, seized my hand and said, "I want to talk with you. I have been to the prayer breakfast every morning this week, and I want to ask you some questions."

There were lines of deep tragedy in his face. I soon found out that his seventeen-year-old son had committed suicide just a few months before, and he told me what this had meant to his wife and himself. As

we talked, he said, "I know I have heard something
this week that must be an answer. I cannot deny that
what I have been hearing all week long in the lives of
these men is real. There is something here, and I
want this. I want to come to Christ, but I cannot
come."

I asked, "Why not?" And he responded, "I do not
feel I can come until I can come in complete honesty.
I have a great deal of doubt and some resentment and
bitterness about what has happened to us, and I don't
think I can come." I said to him, "My dear friend, if
you don't feel you can come honestly, then come dis-
honestly and tell Christ so, for the invitation of the
gospel is, 'Whosoever will, let him come,' that's all,
'let him come.'"

There is in Jesus Christ an adequate answer to *any*
problem. You don't have the answer, but you don't
need to have—*he* does. Bring the problem to him,
whatever it may be: doubt, unbelief, dishonesty,
fear, bitterness, anxiety, worry, *whatever* it is. Remember Jesus said, "Come to me, all who labor and
are heavy laden, and I will give you rest" (Matthew
11:28). And he also said, "All that the Father gives
me will come to me; and him who comes to me I will
not cast out" (John 6:37).

What does he mean? He simply meant that in this
marvelous relationship in which he lived his life on
earth, the Father was forever giving him power over
all flesh, over everyone that came—an adequate answer for every need—so that he in turn, in meeting
that need, might give that man back to the Father,
having received him as a gift of the Father to himself.

Do you see that we stand in exactly the same relationship to the Lord Jesus as he stood to his Father?
Remember these words, "He who believes in me will
also do the works that I do; and greater works than

these will he do, because I go to the Father" (John 14:12). All he is saying is that through the life of Jesus Christ *in us,* he is ready to be continually giving *to us* all power over all flesh. Whatever demand life makes upon us, whatever urgent problem comes bearing down on our lives, he is adequate for it, in order that we might give back to him the rejoicing and the thanksgiving of our hearts.

Major Ian Thomas has reminded us, "We must have what he is in order to do what he did." This is the secret of vital Christianity. Even in this hour of danger and death, when the cross presses with all its confusing bewilderment upon the Lord Jesus, he prays to the Father and says, "Thank you, Father, the hour has come, the hour which will mean the greatest blessing the world has ever seen, the hour for which I have waited, the hour for which I have lived. I know that, in the facing of it, I stand in an adequate relationship which is fully able to meet the demands of that hour."

Intimate Communion

Then there is a third thing with which Jesus introduces this prayer: the unveiling of an unlimited potential. "And this is eternal life, that they know thee the only true God, and Jesus Christ whom thou hast sent" (John 17:3). What does a Christian mean when he testifies that he has eternal life? What is eternal life? Possibly your answer would be, "It means I will live forever." Is that what eternal life really is? Is it nothing but existence, going on and on forever? Is it life spent on Cloud Nine, eternally strumming a harp—is that eternal life? Is it physically walking the golden streets?

No, the definition is right in this verse. Jesus says, *This is eternal life.* What? *That they know thee the only true God, and Jesus Christ whom thou hast sent. That* is eternal life!

Eternal life is not merely quantity, it is quality. It is knowing a person. When you stop to think about it, that is all which makes life worthwhile, isn't it? What is marriage? Is it three meals a day, bathing the children, watching TV, going to sleep, getting up, going to work in the morning? Is that marriage? No, marriage is knowing another person. That is the essence.

It has been a good many years now since I sat in the balcony of a church in Montana one fateful Sunday evening. From the Olympian heights of my seat, I saw a beautiful young girl with long, blonde hair singing a solo. She had the most angelic voice I had ever heard. I said to myself in the impetuosity of youth, "There is the girl I am going to marry." But I felt a terrible sense of frustration, for I was scheduled the next morning to leave for Chicago where I was going to live.

After the meeting was dismissed I met that girl in the doorway of the church, and I asked if I could write to her. I think she was very surprised, but she said yes, and I wrote off and on for five or six years. Eventually I moved to Hawaii, but I was still writing to the same girl. And not long after that I persuaded her to come to Hawaii and we were married.

I had been attempting to know her through correspondence all those years, but I really didn't know her very well until we were married. It was then that we began to know each other, and the whole joy of marriage for me is the knowledge of another person. Marriages which do not have that element in them disintegrate and become nothing but a boring, frustrating experience. It is knowing a person that enriches life.

And that is why eternal life is the knowledge of an eternal Person, the intimacy of communion and fellowship with the Person of God. "This is eternal life, that they may know thee the only true God."

Intended for Life

What are the results of knowledge like that? Whether between humans or between a man and God, they are always the same, except that in the case of knowing God there are no boundaries. The first result is that life becomes enjoyable. Knowing another person means the end of loneliness. It means a sympathizing heart, someone to whom we may tell our problems and who will share our joys and woes. There is no quality in life like it. That is what knowing God is—the fullness of enjoyment, the richest of experiences.

But more than enjoyment, it means enlargement. Have you not observed that someone who is withdrawn from others, who lives a hermit life, either in actual isolation or by being withdrawn and unapproachable, also lives a very narrow life? His life is bounded by fixed habits on the north and unchangeable attitudes on the south—that is the whole of life for him, a narrow grave with both ends kicked out. But when we come to know other persons, and especially when we come to know God, life is enlarged. It takes on breadth as well as length. We discover that the knowledge of God broadens the whole perspective of life until we begin to LIVE for the first time.

On one occasion years ago, I was up on the Canadian border speaking to a group of young adults at a snow conference. After one of the meetings where I had spoken about the knowledge of God, a young man came up to me (I learned later that he was a relatively new convert, a young man who had been a test pilot, and who had lived a rather wild life) and said, "You know, I like that. You are talking about God differently than anyone I have heard before. You don't make him sound like he is off there somewhere. Listening to you I could see that God (and then he groped for a word) . . . God . . . God *swings!"* I must have looked a little mystified, so he added, "Well, you know what I mean. He's with it, God's with it, God swings!"

Now, I understood immediately that there was not the slightest bit of irreverence in what he said. All he was saying (in the youth jargon of that day) was that God is intended for life. He has come to enlarge our lives, and if we do not yield to him, we discover that life becomes a constantly narrowing, restricted channel with no breadth at all.

The knowledge of a person adds enjoyment and enlargement, but most of all, enrichment, for life must not only have length and breadth, but it must also have depth. As we come to know God through Jesus Christ (for there is no other way to the knowledge of God), as we give ourselves to the fellowship and obedience of Jesus Christ, we discover that life becomes enriched by him in all dimensions. He becomes a warm and flaming life within us, and, perhaps for the first time, we begin to experience what human life was intended to be.

One of the men who had helped plan the Newport Beach meetings referred to earlier sat with me at lunch one day and told me the story of his life, how he became a Christian. He had sought for the usual successes of life and had achieved them to a considerable degree. He had all the money he needed, and a fine family.

I shared with him, for his own encouragement, what others had told me about him. And tears came to his eyes as he said, "If what you say is true at all, it is because when I was forty-one years old I discovered Jesus Christ. And I thank God that at forty-one I learned for the first time the true values of life. My father became a Christian only five days before he died, but those last five days were the most wonderful days of his life. I'm simply grateful that though my father only understood the real values of life for five days, I have been permitted for a number of years to realize what life is all about."

That is what the knowledge of God brings. Paul says, "For *all* things are yours, whether . . . the world or life or death or the present or the future, all are yours; and you are Christ's; and Christ is God's" (1 Corinthians 3:21-23). What a magnificent panorama, what tremendous possibilities lie in this simple relationship with Jesus Christ!

Now my question to you is this: Are you praying out of that kind of an understanding, out of that kind of a relationship? Are you seeking to enter into that? Do you really believe that these are the possibilities God is ready to pour into your life? Or are you content, as so many of us are, to plod on week after endless week, doing the same old things with the same attitudes as the worldlings around us, with nothing visibly different in our lives? That is what our Lord confronts us with in this prayer. In the face of the most tragic hour in human history there is nothing of nervousness or defeat in his prayer, but simply a resting upon that which had been the characteristic of his life all along and which he simply says is available for all who believe in him.

Our Father, what pathetic beggars we are, possessing such marvelous riches, enjoying so little of them. Lord, strike away the shackles of our unbe-

lief. Stop us from discounting all this that we hear. Keep us from this terrible thing of going back into "normal life" as we call it, and being the same old person that we were before. God help us to see that in Jesus Christ there is life, and light, and liberty, and abundance, and make us hunger and thirst for them. We pray in his name. Amen.

"I glorified thee on earth, having accomplished the work which thou gavest me to do; and now, Father, glorify thou me in thy own presence with the glory which I had with thee before the world was made. I have manifested thy name to the men whom thou gavest me out of the world; thine they were, and thou gavest them to me, and they have kept thy word. Now they know that everything that thou hast given me is from thee; for I have given them the words which thou gavest me, and they have received them and know in truth that I came from thee; and they have believed that thou didst send me" (John 17:4-8).

10
PRAYER'S
POSSIBILITIES

Suppose you knew that your life would come to an end tomorrow and you wanted to sum up for someone what your life meant, what you felt were the abiding values of your life. What would you say? This is the circumstance in which we find Jesus as we continue in the seventeenth chapter of John.

Earlier, in the thirteenth chapter, which introduces the Upper Room Discourse, John says:

> *Jesus, knowing that the Father had given all things into his hands, and that he had come from God and was going to God, rose from supper, laid aside his garments, and girded himself with a*

> *towel. Then he poured water into a basin, and*
> *began to wash the disciples' feet, and to wipe them*
> *with the towel with which he was girded (John*
> *13:3-5).*

Following that, Jesus spoke to his disciples in the amazing, astonishing words which we call the Upper Room Discourse. When he turns to prayer at the close of the discourse, our Lord reviews his life to the Father, a review of thirty-three years of ministry on earth: those silent years in Nazareth and those action-packed years in his public ministry when he went up and down the hills of Judea and Galilee, preaching and healing and ministering to all the multitudes that followed him.

As we read these words, we are privileged to listen in while he appraises his own life. He is gathering all these thirty-three years into three tremendous statements, which constitute his own evaluation of the greatest life that was ever lived. The first thing he points out to the Father is that *he accomplished a work which glorifies:*

> *I glorified thee on earth, having accomplished the*
> *work which thou gavest me to do; and now,*
> *Father, glorify thou me in thy own presence with*
> *the glory which I had with thee before the world*
> *was made (John 17:4-5).*

Although this prayer was prayed before the cross, in its scope it reaches beyond and includes the cross. Our Lord knew where he was going, he knew what he would be doing in the next few hours and what would be accomplished, and in view of this he says, "I have finished the work which you gave me to do."

Before the World Was Made

That work included more than the cross. It encompassed his ministry of healing and mercy, and as I have suggested, even those thirty silent years back in Nazareth, of which we know so little. They were all part of his life, the work his Father had given him to do. The key to the meaning of this is found in verse five, "Now, Father, glorify thou me in thy own presence [where he was going] with the glory which I had with thee before the world was made."

No other human lips could utter those words. None of us can look back to a time when we were with the Father before the world was made, but here was one who could. And in saying this, he is asking to be restored to the glory that is properly his. If there is any verse in the Bible which singlehandedly and unmistakably reflects the deity of Jesus Christ, it is this verse. For here he is asking for the glory which was the Father's glory as well.

Isaiah reminds us that God does not share his glory with anyone less than himself. "My glory," he says, "I give to no other" (Isaiah 42:8). But here is one who shared the Father's glory before the world was made and who recognizes that it was properly his.

It would be interesting to dwell upon that glory and consider what it was and how he could recall it as a man walking here on the earth, but this is not the point our Lord is making. He brings this up to indicate the character of his work while he was here.

Jesus is suggesting that his work was characterized by a continual self-emptying—a laying aside of glory. Now that he has reached the end he is ready to resume the glory which was properly his, but he is thinking back over thirty-three years of his life and recognizing that all during that time he had voluntarily surrendered his right to be worshiped, his right to the glory that belonged to God.

This brings to mind those words of Paul's in Philippians about Jesus, ". . . who, though he was in the form of God, did not count equality with God a thing to be grasped, but emptied himself [made himself of no reputation, the King James version says] . . . being born in the likeness of men" (Philippians 2:6, 7). Jesus is pointing out that the work that glorified the Father was essentially one of self-emptying. That is what glorifies God!

We are so confused about this. We think that God is interested in our activity, that our religious efforts will be pleasing to him, no matter in what frame of mind we do them. That is why we sometimes drag ourselves out to church, week after week, when we actually have little interest in attending church, because we think that going to church is what God wants. Or we give for some missionary cause because we think this is what God is after.

How little we understand God! It is not activity that he desires. It was not merely that which Jesus *did* which glorified the Father. It was not his ministry of mercy and good works. Others have done similar things. But it was the fact that throughout his life he had a heart that was ready to obey, an ear that was ready to hear, a will that was ready to be subject to the Father. It was his willingness to be always available, to be forever giving of himself, that glorified God.

Think back on this incident at the baptism of Jesus by John when the heavens opened and the voice of the Father came in thunderous tones: "This is my beloved Son, with whom I am well pleased" (Matthew 3:17). He had not done anything yet—that was only the beginning of his ministry—but for thirty years in obscurity he had been delighting the heart of the Father, for during those years, as in all his ministry, he manifested a heart that was ready to obey. That is what glorifies God.

The Cost of Rebellion

There are a great many books on the market written about the so-called "cost of discipleship." They declare in one way or another that in order to have power with God we must pay a high price. In various ways they state that becoming a victorious Christian, an effective Christian, requires a difficult and demanding discipline.

I am not impressed with this type of literature at all because it sets forth a totally negative approach. It puts the cart before the horse. I don't mean that such an approach is not true, for obedience to God does mean saying no to a lot of other things. You cannot say yes to the Spirit of God without, at the same time, saying no to many other things—this is simply inherent in the process of decision. Therefore, I do not mean that power with God and living for the glory of God doesn't cost us certain fancied pleasures and relationships which perhaps we want to hold on to. But the truly costly thing is the cost of disobedience! That is where the emphasis should be put. How well we know *that* cost. What a tremendous toll our disobedience and our unwillingness to give of ourselves takes in our lives. Payment is exacted in terms of frustrated, restless spirits, and shameful, degrading acts that we hope nobody discovers—skeletons that rattle around in our closets for years. Or our lives are depleted through irritated, vexatious dispositions that keep us in a nervous frenzy all the time. But the greatest toll, in some ways, is that of self-righteousness. As a blind for our disobedience, we often rig up a smug religiosity which we call Christianity. This is a stench in the nostrils of the world and an offense to God.

Where do these things come from? Are they not the terrible price that we pay for a rebellious spirit, for an unwillingness to yield ourselves to the Lordship of Christ? *We are not our own,* we say, but we still cling to the right to run our own lives and make our own decisions, to choose our own pleasures, go where we will, do what we want, and we cover it over with pious religiosity! We say we want to do God's will, as long as it is what *we* want to do. At the center of our lives self is still king, and that is the problem. Our own glory is in view. We still want what we want and we are not willing, as Jesus was, to walk in glad obedience even though that is what glorifies the Father.

Let us not talk about living to the glory of God while our own lives are still filled with so much self-centeredness and selfishness. Do you realize that every truly great Christian who ever lived has found that the glory of an obedient life far outweighs the piddling cost of giving up a few selfish desires for Christ's sake? Don't talk about the cost of discipleship; it is the cost of rebellion that we ought to be concerned about.

C. T. Studd, who gave away his fortune and went out into the heart of Africa, said, "If Jesus Christ be God and died for me, then there is no sacrifice too great for me to make for him." David Livingstone said, "I have resolved not to count anything I own of any value, save as it relates to the advance of the Kingdom of God." Was this sacrifice? They would not call it that. Those who have seen the glory of God in an obedient heart never speak of sacrifice. They never talk about what they have given up, because what they have *gotten* is of such tremendous, surpassing value. Paul could say, "Whatever gain I had, I counted as loss for the sake of Christ" (Philippians 3:7). Nothing could compare with what Christ could give to him.

A few years ago they buried a man on a hillside in Korea who was for many years a simple farmer in Oregon. On a trip to the Orient he saw the needs of the desolate, destitute orphans of Korea—those thousands of young children begotten by American soldiers sent to that land. This man saw them as every other tourist who goes to Korea sees them, out in the streets, penniless, begging, no one to care for them.

But unlike the other tourists he did not go on to some other country and forget what he saw. He came home and began to line up homes in America for Korean orphans. He had had one heart attack already, and had been forewarned by his doctor not to over-exert, but he forgot that—he forgot himself and gave himself without stint.

In the week of his death the story of his work appeared in every English language newspaper in the world, for here was a man who had lost himself so that he might glorify God. His name was Harry Holt.

Now as Jesus is talking to the Father, he puts his finger right on the thing that glorifies God, a life of self-giving love. What are we giving ourselves to? Who are we helping?

Next, Jesus reveals the second thing that marks his life: "I have manifested thy name to the men whom thou gavest me out of the world; thine they were, and thou gavest them to me, and they have kept thy word" (John 17:6).

That is an amazing statement, "They have kept thy word." He says, "I have manifested a name that empowers men to keep God's word." There is a relationship between these two. What was the result in the disciples' lives when the name of God became manifest? "They kept thy word."

The Power That Works

Do we not realize that ignorance of the right is seldom our problem? It is not that we do not know what God wants us to do. The truth is, we do not want to do it. In fact, in some way strange to us, we cannot do it; our wills are paralyzed. We may want to, but we cannot.

I will never forget, years ago, a young man with agony in his eyes laying hold of my arm and saying, "What do you do when you know something is wrong and you don't want to do it, but even while you are promising that you won't do it, you know that you are going to do it again? What do you do then?" The only answer I have found to that question is to understand *and to act* on what God is willing to be to us. In other words, to understand the character of God, to lay hold of his name—*that* is the true power of human life and the only power that works.

A name stands for the total character and resources of an individual. My name is all that I am, your name is all that you are. Whatever you are, that is what your name means to others. When my wife took my name in marriage, she literally took me for all I had. It wasn't much! As a matter of fact, we had to cash her bonds to get home from the honeymoon. But whenever I sign my name, "Ray C. Stedman," the whole Stedman fortune, all thirty-five dollars of it, is laid on the line.

Now, the work of Jesus Christ during those thirty-three years of his life was to unveil to us the total resources of the Father, to manifest his name, so that we might discover what a tremendous, unending resource we have in God. We can never get to the bottom of the barrel. Failure to realize this is exactly where our problem of weakness lies. I see Christians struggling, trying to act by faith, and yet all the time sabotaging their efforts by a flat refusal to believe that God is what he says he is.

It is amazing to me how easily we believe the satanic lies about God. We do not believe that God is what he says he is. We believe, essentially, that God is utterly faithless and that he will not do what he says he will do.

When I talk with people and they tell me their troubles, I try to give them advice and counsel. No matter what I suggest, they imply in one way or another that they've tried it without success. They have done everything required, but God does not act, and they have come to believe that he is capricious, a respecter of persons. He will do things for someone else, but he won't do it for them. When we believe that kind of lie, we undermine every effort that God is making to bring us out into victory.

God is faithful. How many times does the Scripture say that?

> *God is faithful, and he will not let you be tempted beyond your strength, but with the temptation will also provide the way of escape, that you may be able to endure it (1 Corinthians 10:13).*

> *God is faithful, by whom you were called into the fellowship of his Son, Jesus Christ our Lord (1 Corinthians 1:9).*

The whole work of Jesus Christ is to show us the faithfulness of God. What a glory is manifested in his life as we see how he rested on God's faithfulness. He was not anxious, he was not troubled, he was not disturbed when the clouds of oppression and persecution began to hang heavy over him, for he rested on the faithful name of God. "The name of the LORD is a strong tower; the righteous man runs into it and is safe" (Proverbs 18:10). Have you discovered that yet?

There is yet a third thing Jesus said characterized his life: ". . . for I have given them the words which thou gavest me, and they have received them and know in truth that I came from thee; and they have believed that thou didst send me" (John 17:8).

What made these Jewish disciples, who were mortally afraid of idolatry, believe that this man with whom they had lived, eaten, and slept, with whom they had walked the roads of Galilee and Judea, whom they had seen in all the weakness of his human life—what made them believe that this *man,* in all his humanity, was also incarnate God, sent of the Father?

John could write: "In the beginning was the Word, and the Word was with God, and the Word was God" (John 1:1). How did he learn that? Was it Jesus' miracles that convinced him? No, his miracles never convinced anyone of his deity. They convinced them of his Messiahship; that is what they were designed to do. Was it the power that he exercised over men? No, there have been evil men that have exercised tremendous power over the minds and hearts of men. It wasn't that. What was it?

It was his words! The words of Jesus searched their hearts, opened their eyes, dispelled their doubts, and set their lives afire. They knew that when they took these words seriously, things happened to them that only God could do. Gradually, through the course of three and one-half years, as they listened to those compelling, magnetic words, there was born in their hearts the faith that here was One who came from God. "They have received them and know in truth that I come from thee; and they have believed that thou didst send me."

To Awaken Faith

The words of Jesus still have that power today. Are you troubled by doubts as to your Christian faith? In these days when there is so great an attack against the foundations of faith, it wouldn't be surprising if you were. If you are troubled with doubts, may I suggest something? Start reading the words of Jesus and take them seriously. Don't just read them, take them as a revelation of basic underlying truth. Take them seriously. You won't read far before discovering so much understanding of life and experience that you cannot help believing that these words are indeed the words of God.

What pitiful groping exists among Christians today. I am troubled by the way young theologians, new graduates of seminaries, frankly admit that they are better acquainted with the writings of Tillich, Barth, and Bultmann than they are with the writings of Moses and Paul. No wonder they have weak foundations for their faith. Nothing convinces like the matchless Word of God.

Here are the three things that Jesus came to do. He said, I came to give myself in a self-emptying ministry; I came to manifest an all-empowering Name by which anything that needs to be done may be done; and I came to speak compelling words that would awaken faith in men's hearts and cause them to believe. John said at the beginning of this discourse that Jesus knew the Father had given all things into his hands. He knew that he had come from God, and he knew that he was going to God, and in between lay those thirty-three years whose impact the world can never escape, which he is gathering up in these three brief phrases: a work accomplished, a name manifested, and words uttered to awaken faith. He came from God and he went to God. That is a Christian life.

Now tell me, where did you get your Christian life? Did you have it when you were born into this world? Of course not, you got it when you believed in Jesus Christ. It came from God. It was with the Father before you received it because it was in Jesus Christ. This life is in his Son. "He who has the Son has life; he who has not the Son of God has not life" (1 John 5:12).

What happens to your life when you get through with it here on earth? Where does it go? Every Christian believes it goes to the Father. "My desire is to depart and be with Christ, for that is far better," says Paul (Philippians 1:23). So these words are true of you, as well. It came from God, it goes to God.

And what is in between? A life that glorifies the Father, manifesting before the world the name that empowers men, and speaking words that grip them and bring them to a realization of their own need and to an understanding of truth and reality.

Jesus offers a prayer here that includes all of us, and the astonishing thing is that there is not a word that you and I cannot pray as well. May God lead us to lay hold of the transforming, dynamic Christian life that Jesus himself manifested.

> *Oh Father, these words of the Lord Jesus search us, they reveal to us things that we have never known before, mighty facts, so awesome that we can scarcely believe them. But Lord, help us to remember where they come from and thus that they are true, and to stand upon them with boldness and confidence. Keep us from being ineffective, ordinary Christians; challenge us individually, one by one, to be among those who are ready to fling our lives*

away for Jesus Christ, to be utterly careless of what happens to us in order that he may be glorified. We pray in his name, Amen.

"I am praying for them; I am not praying for the world but for those whom thou hast given me, for they are thine; all mine are thine, and thine are mine, and I am glorified in them. And now I am no more in the world, but they are in the world, and I am coming to thee. Holy Father, keep them in thy name, which thou hast given me, that they may be one, even as we are one. While I was with them, I kept them in thy name, which thou hast given me; I have guarded them, and none of them is lost but the son of perdition, that the scripture might be fulfilled. But now I am coming to thee; and these things I speak in the world, that they may have my joy fulfilled in themselves. I have given them thy word; and the world has hated them because they are not of the world, even as I am not of the world. I do not pray that thou shouldst take them out of the world, but that thou shouldst keep them from the evil one. They are not of the world, even as I am not of the world. Sanctify them in the truth; thy word is truth. As thou didst send me into the world, so I have sent them into the world. And for their sake I consecrate myself, that they also may be consecrated in truth" (John 17:9-19).

11
CHRIST PRAYS
FOR YOU

As Jesus prepared to leave his disciples and move on to the cross, they felt frightened, helpless, alone, and unable to understand what was taking place. They could not see that our Lord was merely introducing a higher and better relationship to them. Do we not feel this way? God leads us to a place of change and we are frightened by it. We wonder if we are not losing everything we held dear in the past. We scarcely realize that God is only leading us to a higher, newer, and greater relationship. Like these disciples we are frightened and fearful.

As we come to our study of these words in John 17:9-19, my concern is how to convey something of the gripping reality of the requests of Jesus—something of the intense practicality of what Jesus is saying. I am so afraid that we will listen to these words as we would to beautiful poetry or a moving drama, and, entranced by their familiarity and beauty, fail to realize that Jesus is actually praying for us here—for what he prays for his disciples he prays for us.

This prayer ought to hit us like a punch in the jaw. Or, perhaps, like a hand that grabs us as we are going down for the third time. These words ought both to sober us and comfort us. They are not soft, beautiful words, prayed in a great cathedral, but earthy, gutty words, uttered on a battlefield in which our Lord is coming to grips with evil as it really is, and as such they ought to strike that note of reality with us.

Keep Them

The first thing that arrests our attention is the *plea* that Jesus utters for his disciples: "Holy Father, keep them" (John 17:11). Later he said, "I do not pray that thou shouldst take them out of the world, but that thou shouldst keep them . . ." (John 17:15). This is the theme of his prayer: that they might be kept.

Why? There are so many things that I would pray for if I were in his place (if any man could be in his place). They are the usual things we pray for one another: "Use them," "strengthen them," "teach them," or "guide them." But now that he is leaving them, he wants to put into one brief phrase all that is his heart's urging and desire for them, and he sums it up in those two little words, "Keep them!"

As I thought it through, I found that this is what I pray when I am about to leave my family or when I am away from them. When I am with my loved ones, I can pray more specifically for them, but when I am away, I am continually praying, "Lord, keep them, keep them." All of this simply points up the fact which is highlighted for us here in this prayer of Jesus that relationship is the supreme thing. Whom we are with is far more important than what we do. Whom you fellowship with determines what you are, so Jesus' prayer is that their relationship with the Father remain intact, for from that relationship everything else he desires will come. So he prays, "Keep them."

As he prays, our Lord has in view the *peril* in the world; he says,

> *I have given them thy word; and the world has hated them because they are not of the world, even as I am not of the world. I do not pray that thou shouldst take them out of the world, but that thou shouldst keep them from the evil one (John 17:14-15).*

Our Lord saw very clearly into the nature of life as it is, the nature of reality. He realizes that Christians, believers, are facing a hostile world, behind which there is a sinister being of incredible subtlety whom we call the devil. We do not see him; it would be helpful if we could. He would be much more easily dealt with if he were visible, but unfortunately he is not. He keeps himself behind the scenes, and thus has created the myth that he does not even exist. But in the eyes of Jesus, who saw things as they really were, the devil was a very real being. And while as human beings, we cannot see the devil, we are able to see his front, which Jesus calls "the world."

Christians have struggled with this problem of the world and have wondered what it means all through the twenty centuries of this Christian age. There are some who have made the mistake of thinking it is the world of nature and that Christians ought not to have anything to do with the enjoyment of natural

beauty—the glories of the mountains and the sea—
the whole world of natural life. This is certainly not
true. Others have wondered if it means the world of
natural relationships, our family life, friends, home,
the relationships between mothers and fathers and
children. No, this is not "the world" of which our
Lord warns. The term "world," as it is used here,
means preeminently the basic assumptions which
men and women make who live without God; in
other words, a secular philosophy of life.

Worldliness Unmasked

Some time ago I received an invitation to subscribe
to a magazine that was, I felt, extremely worldly. It
was a new publication and, as I read the prospectus, it
seemed to me that this magazine would speak forth-
rightly along the line of worldly philosophy. I sub-
scribed to it for that reason, and my anticipations
were fulfilled completely. As I read it, I discovered
that here was worldliness blatantly, boldly set
forth—worldliness unmasked! But actually, the phi-
losophies reflected in this publication are detectable
in almost any popular magazine published today.
The same ideas underlie most television and radio
broadcasts, but seldom are they as boldly stated as in
this particular sheet. I read through two issues and
jotted down a few statements to illustrate what I
mean. From one article these words are taken:

> *It is the moralists who are responsible for our pres-
> ent level of sex crime and the state of affairs re-
> vealed in the Kinsey Report. The world is sick with
> morality.*

> *The problems of poverty and racial injustice and
> political corruption and everything else, are all
> branches of a single evil tree, and that tree is Au-*

thority. Obedience to authority is the one single principle that explains every evil in human history.

The Freudian concepts of sex-motivation can adequately explain all human phenomena.

Organized religion is a tough old rooster which has traditionally been first in the American pecking-order. The press can peck the government, the government can peck industry, industry can peck labor, and labor can peck all three of them back, but nobody can peck the rooster and the rooster can always peck anyone else at any time with impunity.

The problem, they say, is the Church.

I gathered these to document what Jesus says: the world hates his disciples because they are not of the world. The world in which we live is dominated by a satanic philosophy which is diametrically opposed to all that God stands for. We make a very serious mistake when we forget that fact and try to settle down in this world and become comfortable in it as though this were the climate in which we ought to feel at home.

Perhaps the most effective propaganda of the world is the satanic lie that we call "romanticism." There are millions fooled by it, though it is nothing more than a lie. Certainly many of our young people are profoundly influenced by this idea. It is the illusion that life is intended to be all moonlight and roses, swashbuckling adventure, or breath-taking journeys to faraway places. Look over the nearest magazine stand and you will see what I mean. Nearly all the magazines make their appeal along the lines of romance, of body building, adventure and health, or of travel and excitement. There is the world in all its

silken delusion, luring, beckoning with soft music
and dim lights and exotic names and places.

It is rather easy to lose one's head and sell out for
"the good life," which, unfortunately, is never discovered. It is a bitter irony of our day, perhaps more
than in any other age, that by giving ourselves to the
pursuit of dreams offered by our new gadgetry, we
never find the good life they promise. When we have
surrounded ourselves with all that our dreams have
envisaged, we find our lives are still empty and purposeless, without meaning, because "the good life" is
all a dream, a fantasy, a web of deceit, promising
much but delivering nothing.

The Christian answer to romanticism is in John
17:13: ". . . I am coming to thee; and these things I
speak in the world, that they may have my joy fulfilled in themselves." There is where joy lies, and fulfillment, and meaning, and purpose, and blessing;
not in pursuing the will-o'-the-wisp of romantic adventure or in seeking satisfaction in material things,
but in a life and heart that is committed to Jesus
Christ, which knows him and fellowships with him.
Here indeed is a style of life filled with an unexplainable joy that simply cannot be compared with anything else.

A few years ago I heard a man say, "I have had so
much fun in my life that I can hardly describe it. Life,
to me, has been a continually exciting thing." Who
was that? Was it someone who has given himself to
the search for adventure? No, that man was Dr.
Frank Laubach who, as a Christian, lost himself in
the cause of trying to teach people all over the world
to read so they would be able to read the words of life
and truth in Scripture. A young man said in my presence not long ago, "I am a radio physicist. I work on
the frontiers of the exciting world of science, explor-

ing the universe. But I must say that this exciting realm of science in which I work seems to be dull business indeed compared to the excitement that comes from knowing Jesus Christ."

A Supernatural Task

From whence comes this power that keeps us straight when the world with its allurement and pressures surrounds us as an ambient sea? When we are enveloped in a total climate of deceit, how can we keep our heads? How can we be kept? The only possible answer is the power that our Lord counts on here. He pinpoints it twice; "Keep them Father, *in thy name.*" And later, "While I was with them, I kept them *in thy name.*"

As we have already seen, the name of God stands for all the authority and resources of God. What Jesus is saying here is that keeping a believer from the allurements and the deceit of the world is a supernatural task. No man is smart enough to do it on his own—only the power of God can keep us. This is reflected throughout the Epistles of the New Testament. Paul said, "I know whom I have believed, and I am sure that he is able to guard . . ." and it does not make any difference whether you translate the next phrase "what has been entrusted to me" or "what I have entrusted to him" (2 Timothy 1:12). Either translation is possible, but in any case, God is able to keep. Peter speaks of those "who by God's power are guarded through faith for a salvation ready to be revealed in the last time" (1 Peter 1:5). And almost the last promise of Scripture is that word of Jude's, "Now to him who is able to keep you from falling and to present you without blemish before the presence of his glory with rejoicing . . ." (Jude 24). Nothing else will suffice.

To highlight this, Jesus spotlights for us the one apparent exception when he says, "I have guarded them, and none of them is lost but the son of perdition, that the scripture might be fulfilled" (John 17:12). What a sobering, frightening possibility is revealed here in Judas. Here is a man who was one of the disciples, called by Jesus Christ, included in the intimate, inner circle of the twelve, a highly religious man—obviously so—a man who was dedicated to the cause of God as he saw it. He was a moral man in many ways, though he was not above a little pilfering from the bag now and then—a sincere, earnest man of strong convictions and powerful drives.

But there was one thing wrong with Judas, only one. He thought he could keep himself by his own efforts. He thought he could do it on his own. He thought he could follow Christ in his own strength and use him for his own ends. Judas had never made that inner surrender of the heart by which he recognized his utter weakness and cast himself on Christ. He had never come to the place of saying, as we sing in that old hymn, "Nothing in my hand I bring, simply to thy cross I cling." He had never come to Christ, desperately aware of his own weakness, as the other disciples had. "Lord, to whom shall we go? You have the words of eternal life," Peter said (John 6:68). "You are a disturbing man to live with. Other teachers make their appeal to us, but Lord, to whom can we go? No one else, no one else can do what you can do."

Judas did not become the son of perdition when he betrayed Jesus; he was the son of perdition all along. He never was anything else. He never was in the Father's keeping power, and so the Father could not keep him. But those who have learned not to trust themselves, who have, as Paul says, "no confidence in the flesh," are kept by the Father's name and nothing, Jesus says, nothing—NOTHING—can separate them from the Father's love. "No one is able to snatch them out of the Father's hand" (John 10:29). He keeps them.

A Part for Us

Perhaps some of you are saying, "Isn't there any part for us?" Yes, there is, and it is both the easiest and the hardest thing in the world. Look at the program that he unfolds for us:

> *Sanctify them in the truth; thy word is truth. As thou didst send me into the world, so I have sent them into the world. And for their sake I consecrate {or "I sanctify," it is the same word} myself, that they also may be consecrated in truth (John 17:17-19).*

Now there is that troublesome word: "sanctification." What does it mean? I do not know of any word in the Scripture that is more misunderstood. Many tend to regard sanctification as a sort of de-worming process, a kind of religious sheep-dip, necessary to make us usable. No, it simply means "to put to the proper use," that is all. I am sanctifying a microphone when I use it to amplify my voice. I am sanctifying the pulpit when I preach. You are sanctifying the chairs you are sitting on; you are simply putting them to their proper use.

When Jesus says to the Father, "Father, sanctify them," he means, "Lord, make these men and women fulfill the ideal that you have for them. Put them to their proper use. Let them find the reason they were born. Bring them to the place where they discover your program for them." How? By the truth: "thy word is truth."

Now this brings us to our part. In all this mighty
program of God, what is our part? It is simply to believe the truth. At this moment some of you are no
doubt sighing to yourself and saying, "Oh, it's the
same old stuff. That's what they say all the time."
And that is true, that *is* what we say all the time. But
evidently one of the most difficult things for human
hearts to do is simply to believe that what God has
written is the truth regardless of what our feelings
may be.

The brutal fact is that we much prefer to believe
our feelings than the Word. That is where our problem lies. More than once, Christians have said to me,
"I simply cannot take it any longer, I give up. Scripture does not seem to work for me. I try to fulfill the
promises, I try to rely on the Lord, I try to appropriate Christ, I try to do all these things, but it does not
work for me. It may work for you, but it does not
work for me. I cannot take the pressures that come, I
cannot take the testings that I am subjected to." And
I remind them of what Paul says, "No temptation has
overtaken you that is not common to man" (1 Corinthians 10:13). I say, "Now don't get discouraged.
You are not going through anything that others have
not gone through." And almost inevitably the reac-
tion is, "That cannot be, nobody else has gone
through what I am going through! I simply cannot
believe that what I am going through is a common
experience. The trouble is, you do not understand
what I am going through, nobody understands, no
one!"

Now that is nothing more than disguised unbelief—a refusal to take what God says as the truth.
There is the problem. We say we believe, but we do
not believe, because when it comes down to the actual application of it we really mean, "God is a liar,

my feelings are what is true! The way I feel, that is fact."

Follow All Directions

Supposing one of you should ask, "How do you go about traveling by an airplane? I have never flown before. Tell me how it is done." In response, a friend replies, "Well, it is very simple. You simply call the airline that goes to the destination you desire and make a reservation. Then you arrange to buy the ticket and you present that ticket at the proper time at the airport and you will be admitted to the plane. You then go aboard, sit down, and fasten your seatbelt—the plane does all the rest!" "But," you reply, "I am not sure that I understand what you mean. Write it out for me, will you?" So the other person writes, "Make a reservation; buy the ticket; present it at the proper time; get aboard the plane; that is all."

A couple of days later you come around and say, "Well, I tried it, but it doesn't work. I made the reservation, bought the ticket, went down to the airport, and do you know what they told me? They said the plane left two hours ago! It doesn't work!" To this, the other person replies, "Wait a minute. Remember, I said in the instructions, present the ticket at the proper time. Did you do that?"

"Oh," you respond, "I read that, but I didn't think it had any particular importance. After all, one time is as good as another. I went when I was ready." And your friend then says, "Well, there is your trouble. If you are going to act on any of the instructions, you must act on all of them. You cannot leave out any part. If you fail in one part, it cancels out the whole of the program. You did not go at the proper time, therefore it didn't work for you."

Now that simple analogy, crude though it may be, is a very accurate parallel to what frequently goes on in our Christian experience. We must believe that God has told us the truth. There is no value in Christian faith at all if we do not believe that. If the Bible is nothing more than another voice among the thousands that blare at us all week long giving advice and counsel, then it is utterly worthless. But here *is* the revelation of truth, of things as they are, regardless of how we feel. We shall never make any progress in our spiritual lives until we come to grips with the fact that what God says is true. As Paul says, "Let God be true though every man be false" (Romans 3:4). When we start believing what he says as truth, and act upon it, we discover that all that he says is gloriously and marvelously confirmed.

It is true that God protects us and keeps us even when our faith fails; thank God for that. He is the Author and the Finisher of faith, and our faith rests upon the foundation of his faithfulness, but it is also true that we will never go any farther than our faith takes us. God may awaken faith anew in us, but we can never make any progress, we can never lay hold of any truth, we can never appropriate any blessing that does not come through the door of a quiet, trustful belief in what God says.

Therefore, Jesus prays, "Sanctify them, put them to the proper use, let them discover what life is all about, by the truth; thy word is truth. On this basis," Jesus says, "I myself have been operating. As thou hast sent me into the world, to live by a continual appropriating of thy power, available because I believe what thou hast said, so I have sent them into the world. I have given them an example. I have sanctified myself in front of their eyes by this same process of believing the truth, despite all the conflicting evidence of my senses. I have sanctified myself, that they also may be sanctified, consecrated in the truth."

Our Father, we pray that the words that we have been reading here may not simply be words of beauty, but may we come to grips with them and see them as words of practical counsel—the most practical setting forth of the way to the experience we long for of victory and power and blessing in Jesus Christ our Lord. Lord, teach us to turn a deaf ear to the siren voice of the world about us which seeks to delude us, but may we open our ears fully, completely, to this wonderful, truthful voice, this voice of reality from your word that tells us what life is truly like. And as we step forth upon it, we thank you, Father, that the confirmation to our heart is one of incredible, unexplainable joy. For that we give thanks in Christ's name, Amen.

"I do not pray for these only, but also for those who believe in me through their word, that they may all be one; even as thou, Father, art in me, and I in thee, that they also may be in us, so that the world may believe that thou hast sent me. The glory which thou hast given me I have given to them, that they may be one even as we are one, I in them and thou in me, that they may become perfectly one, so that the world may know that thou hast sent me and hast loved them even as thou hast loved me. Father, I desire that they also, whom thou hast given me, may be with me where I am, to behold my glory which thou hast given me in thy love for me before the foundation of the world. O righteous Father, the world has not known thee, but I have known thee; and these know that thou hast sent me. I made known to them thy name, and I will make it known, that the love with which thou hast loved me may be in them, and I in them" (John 17:20-26).

12
THE PRAYER
FOR UNITY

We have already seen something of the possibilities, the priorities, and the perils of the Christian life reflected in our Lord's prayer for us, but in the last six verses of the prayer are found the most unusual of all. Here is what we may view as a great planning session between the Father, Son, and Holy Spirit, and we are privileged to listen. This is, in other words, a summit meeting—the highest possible summit.

It does not focus on a single country or continent of the world, but it takes in the entire world. The purpose of the summit is not to plan a campaign of a few years or a decade or two. Rather, it encompasses the entire age in which we live, from the first coming of

Christ to the second coming. It does not involve a few local churches or a denomination or two in some kind of united campaign, but it gathers in the whole body of Christ—every Christian who has ever lived or ever will live in all time. In a very real sense these verses are the key to history, the blueprints of God's program for this age. From another viewpoint, this is the plan of a military campaign which is designed to recapture this rebellious planet for God. A number of years ago a British army major taught me the three essentials of military planning: an objective, strategy, and tactics, and he explained the difference between them. The objective is the goal, the hilltop you wish to take or the city that needs to be captured. The strategy is the general procedure, the overall plan by which it is proposed to take the objective, and the tactics are the specific maneuvers by which the strategy is carried out. Every military campaign must include all three of these.

Bull's-eye: the World

Now, in this prayer of Jesus which, as I have suggested, was not prayed in a quiet sanctuary but on a battlefield, you have the three ingredients of a military campaign.

You can see this in these six verses by looking closely. Twice in this section, Jesus states the great objective which was constantly before him as he lived his own life on earth, and now that he is leaving, he is committing it to the disciples. Twice he outlines specifically what God intends to accomplish. In the latter part of John 17:21, he says ". . . so that the world may believe that thou hast sent me"; and again in the latter part of verse twenty-three, ". . . so that the world may know that thou hast sent me." There is the great objective. God's whole redemptive plan is aimed at one target: the world. "God so loved the world that he gave his only Son, that whoever believes in him should not perish but have eternal life" (John 3:16). It is so easy for Christians to forget this. Forgetting that we were once part of this world, we become so absorbed in his work in us as believers that we sometimes forget that he is still aiming beyond us.

We seem to feel that God's program stops with us, that his entire purpose in coming into the world and leaving by the cross and the resurrection is to get us to heaven. If that were so, it would be much simpler to erect a chopping block in every church, and as soon as someone becomes a Christian, chop his head off! We could be sure then that they would get to heaven without any difficulty!

But it is clear from the Scriptures that this is not the Lord's plan. He leaves us here in order that we may learn how to share in the painful process of drawing a struggling, rebellious creation to himself. We must become part of the process of reaching the world.

It should be understood, however, that we Christians are not here essentially to improve the world. Sometimes we become so concerned about necessary social changes that we give the impression that the Church exists in order to make the world a better place in which to live. But that misses the point entirely, for the whole picture given by Scripture is that no matter what the Church does, as God's instrument in the world, the ultimate end of the world will be anarchy and chaos. It will end exactly as Jesus Christ described it, despite the best efforts of the Church, and it was never intended otherwise. No, the Church is not here to improve the world, least of all to save the world. We are here for but one thing, and Jesus says it here: "That the world may believe that thou, Father, hast sent me."

An Opportunity to Choose

The Church is left here so that worldlings may become convinced that Jesus Christ is the authentic voice of God; that he is the authoritative word concerning what God intends to do in human affairs; that he is the key to world history and reality; that he is the revelation of the invisible God and the only way from man to God. When the world becomes convinced of this, the rest is up to them. Our task, as believers in Jesus Christ, is not to save the world; our job is to bring it to an awareness of him so that worldlings will do one of two things: will either accept him and be saved, or reject him and continue in the lost condition in which the whole world exists.

While attending a missionary conference in Pasadena, California, several years ago, I attended a session in which a panel of missionaries and mission leaders were being questioned. One of the questions asked was, "What is the definition of world evangelism?" Several answers were given, but the one which impressed me most was: "World evangelism is the attempt to give every man an opportunity to make an intelligent choice of whether to receive or reject Jesus Christ." Excellent, that is exactly what world evangelism is.

Therefore, for the sake of a confused and sinful world which is facing enormously complex problems, Christians must not, dare not, isolate themselves from that world. It is the very thing we are here to reach—that is the goal, the target, the objective. We dare not live out our Christian lives in air-tight compartments, limited only to Christian friends, in a sort of Christian hothouse.

No, the Church is here to be God's instrument by which human life, in every area and at every level, is penetrated by the transforming gospel of Jesus Christ. The mission of the Church is that men may see that Jesus Christ is the authentic voice of God to men; that in him is the ultimate issue of human destiny, and in him we come face to face with all that is important in human affairs.

I have already suggested that this is a complex, difficult, and painful problem, for we well know, having once been on the other side of the fence, that every worldling lives in confusion and blindness. He is suspicious and sensitive—especially in religious matters. Today's worldling loves to remind us of what he considers a major rule of life: Never discuss politics or religion. He may retreat under a hard shell of indifference and sophistication and be apparently unreachable. Yet that man is our objective. Regardless of what attitudes or defenses we may encounter, our objective is to reach every man and woman, every boy and girl, giving each an opportunity to make an intelligent choice to accept or refuse Jesus Christ.

Divine Strategy

Well, if that is the objective, what is the strategy? How does God plan to accomplish this? He has not given us the objective and left the strategy up to us. No, it is here too. Look at the divine strategy as Jesus declares it: *"that they may all be one;* even as thou, Father, art in me, and I in thee, that they also may be in us, *so that* the world may believe that thou hast sent me" (John 17:21). And again, Jesus says, "I in them and thou in me, that they may become perfectly one, *so that* the world may know that thou hast sent me . . ." (John 17:23).

There it is, "That they may become perfectly one." That is the strategy by which God intends to accomplish his objective.

There are those who tell us that this prayer of Jesus concerning the church—"that they may be one"— must now begin to be answered. They believe that now is the time, after twenty centuries of its remaining unfulfilled, to forget all the differences and distinctions that have separated us into various denominations and sectarian groups and join in one great organization or union.

But is this prayer really unanswered today? Can it be possible for twenty centuries to roll by before God the Father begins to fulfill this last request of Jesus? Is it possible that the World Council of Churches will succeed where God the Father has failed? No, this prayer has been answered ever since the day of Pentecost. This strategy is not of human making. The business of making all Christians one does not depend upon us, it depends upon the Spirit of God. He came for that purpose. Paul's great chapter on the Holy Spirit in 1 Corinthians clearly establishes the fact that in his coming he accomplished what Jesus prayed for. This is the divine strategy by which the world may be led to believe.

All Christians *are* one, not in union, as is being suggested today, but in unity. There is a difference. Union is an outward agreement, an alliance, formed by the submerging of differences for the sake of merging. There is much of it going on today. Almost every month the papers carry a report of denominational groups that are considering merging. But is this artificial union, this joining into one organization, the answer to Jesus' prayer, "that they may all be one"? Does it do what Jesus says will be accomplished when the church is one? Does it, in other words, cause worldlings to believe that Jesus is the authentic voice of God? In observing the world scene today, there is little or no evidence that this is the case. My observation is that when churches or denominations join (though there may be good in much of this; do not misunderstand me, I certainly am not decrying all that is involved in these efforts), it creates a vast monolithic power structure which causes men and women of the world to fear the church as a threat to their own power structures. It becomes a rival force in world politics and world affairs.

Unity: Sharing the Life

This type of union doesn't always create oneness. When I was in Formosa a few years ago, I was tremendously impressed by the remarkable oneness among the American missionaries, despite their denominational differences. At the great missionary conferences held once a year at Sun Moon Lake, high in the mountains of Formosa, all the missionaries of the island, I think without exception, gather together for a fellowship time. The denominations represented span the entire spectrum of Christian life today, from the Mennonites (who appeared in colorful uniforms) to the more liberal churches and denominations. But the thing that impressed me was that, as they gathered together, there was a wonderful sense of oneness, of unity in the Lord, a glorious, heavenlike atmosphere. Later a strong effort was made to join all the groups into one organization. What was the result? They lost their wonderful unity.

But unity, as indicated in our Scripture text, is the sharing of a life. Look at verse twenty-one again: "that they may all be one; even as thou, Father, art in me, and I in thee." This is not alliance, nor merger, nor agreement; it is the sharing of life, which is quite a different matter. In the Lord's divine strategy he intends to bring the world a family life, a shared life, so that men and women all over the earth, in becoming members of that life by the new birth, enter a family circle which is so unmistakable and so filled with joy and warmth that worldlings will envy it. Like homeless orphans with their noses pressed up against the window, they will long to join the warmth and the fellowship of the family circle. When the church is like this, there is no evangelistic thrust that is more potent.

I once attended a men's retreat to which one man came who was evidently not yet a Christian. As far as I knew, he was the only one. He told us that he was embittered against the church, he was suspicious of the Scriptures, and he was committed in his life to bad habits which he recognized were not acceptable in Christian circles. He came with all his defenses and barriers in position, but it was evident, as the weekend went on, that he could not resist the warmth of the Christian love expressed among the men who were there. It was not surprising, therefore, that before the weekend closed, he too joined the family circle of God. He could not stay away; all his defenses melted in the presence of Christian oneness. There, you see, is the divine strategy—to make all Christians share one life in one great family and so make the world, starving for meaningful personal relationships, simply drool with desire. That is God's strategy.

The Glory Is Love

But unity is hard to see. The life of Jesus Christ in the body of Christ is an invisible thing. Something must make it visible. But what? Now we come to the divine tactics by which God intends to implement his strategy. What are they? Jesus tells us in John 17:22: "The glory which thou hast given me I have given to them, that they may be one . . ."

The world will believe when they see that the church is one, and this is what makes them one, "the glory which thou hast given me." Look at verse twenty-four: "Father, I desire that they also, whom thou hast given me, may be with me where I am [that is not a reference to glory 'some day,' but to what Paul says in Ephesians, 'we are now seated in heavenly places'; sharing what he is], to behold my glory which thou hast given me in thy love for me before the foundation of the world." Here is a glory, a flaming glory in the church which makes the unity of believers visible. What is it? Jesus is very specific: "I made known to them thy name, and I will make it known, that the love with which thou hast loved me may be in them, and I in them" (v. 26).

The glory is love! In other words, the unity of the church is visible when Christians love one another. There is the whole secret.

In saying that we put our finger squarely on the reason for the failure of the church to reach the world in our day. Why are we seeing this remarkable upsurge of blatant attacks against the Christian faith? Why, in this day of ours, is there widespread apathy to biblical authority, an indifferent unconcern of the world at large to hear the voice of the church?

Is it only coincidence that the decades before this were preeminently characterized by church conflict, that during those years the world saw Christians hurling invectives at one another and splitting theological hairs with ecclesiastical razor blades and then splitting over the splits? Newspapers and magazines were published that were devoted to name-calling and heresy-hounding. They devoted their energies to fighting one another rather than proclaiming the gospel of Jesus Christ. Is it any wonder that the world has turned a deaf ear to the church?

Charles Spurgeon spoke of those who habitually go about with a theological revolver in their ecclesiastical trousers. We still have them with us today. This is why Jesus, gathering here with his disciples in the Upper Room, in one final word said, "A new commandment I give to you, that you love one another" (John 13:34). Here is the key: that you love one another. There is where world evangelization must start! These are the tactics by which the divine strategy is implemented to reach the great objective "that the world may believe that thou hast sent me."

This is why Jesus said, "By this all men will know that you are my disciples, if you have love for one another" (John 13:35). More than that, John says, "He who loves God should love his brother also" (1 John 4:21). It all begins there. And this love is not to be mere sentiment, which has been described as "that warm feeling about the heart that you can't scratch." Nor is it something with which to disguise a dagger of dislike. The Scripture says "let love be unfeigned"; that is, let it be genuine.

The Love That Shows

There are three essential qualities to genuine Christian love. The first one is mutual *contact*. It is simply hogwash to speak of loving another Christian to whom you will not speak. There must be contact, the willingness to talk, with no aloofness, no withdrawal from each other. Now there are certain clearly described circumstances involving discipline where Christians are to withdraw temporarily from one another, but those are very specific and only under unusual circumstances.

But we are to love each other simply because we are Christians, and we are not to be selective about it. It isn't "our kind" of Christian, our specific group that we are to love—the ones that we feel something in common with. That kind of love is what the world employs. Jesus said, "If you salute only your brethren, what more are you doing than others?" (Matthew 5:47). No, we are to love all of them simply because they are Christians, whether they are stupid or wrong or irritating or stubborn. Contact is first.

Second, genuine love involves mutual *concern*. By that I do not mean some superficial greeting in passing, "How are you getting along these days?" but a willingness to listen to the answer. Every contact is to be marked by a readiness to help, to share, to listen, to pray—a willingness to bear one another's burdens in the Lord and so fulfill the law of Christ.

And third, all true Christian love is marked by a mutual sense of *contribution*. That means a recognition that we need each other, that we are not condescending when we give ourselves to another Christian. You have what another one needs, he has what you need, and we minister to one another, young and old alike. Some of the most helpful lessons I have ever learned have come to me from new babes in Christ with whom I have fellowshiped. They have taught me much. We need one another.

It is significant that every great awakening throughout the whole course of Christian history has invariably begun by a breaking down of the barriers between Christians. When longstanding feuds have been resolved and apologies have been made; when pardons have been sought, confessions have been uttered, and a breaking down of dislikes and disagreements, separations and withdrawals occur among Christian people, it is inevitably followed by the world around sitting up and beginning to take notice of the Christian message. Now that is love: contact, concern, contribution.

Let me add one thing more, because this love, as we recognize so clearly from the Scriptures, is not something we work up. It is given to us. It is in us by the very virtue of the fact that Jesus Christ is in us, but it does require our *consent*. The Lord is ready to love another through us anytime we are ready to let ourselves be the channel of that love. That is the whole position of Scripture. When we are ready to consent to love, he is quite ready to love. The thing that makes the Spirit heard and seen in his thrusting urge to reach the blinded and confused world outside is that we give willing, glad consent to love any Christian, any time, for Jesus' sake.

I have resolved that my heart shall be always ready to love every person, without exception, in whom I sense a love for Jesus Christ, the Son of God—regardless of his denominational label or lack of it and despite any theological differences of viewpoint. I am ready, God in me and helping me, to give myself in love to any Christian, anywhere, whom I may chance to meet and in whom I sense a fellowship of love for Jesus Christ. That is the basis for Christian unity.

Are you willing to join in that? Are you ready now to say, in order to reach the world around us, Lord teach me to give up my prejudices, these separations, this withdrawal, these sub-Christian attitudes toward my fellow brethren in Christ and make me willing to love them and to show it for Christ's sake?

Father, you are the God of love. When we look at the cross of our Lord Jesus Christ, we see that love poured out for us. What remarkable love that is, love that will not let us go, love that pursues us despite our rebuffs, love that never gives up, is relentless in its pursuit until we yield, broken, melted by your love. Lord, this is the nature and character of the love that is shed abroad in our hearts by the Holy Spirit which is given unto us. It is this remarkable thing that the world waits to see in Christian people. It is the absence of this, Father, that makes them turn away from our doors, uninterested, disappointed. Lord, teach us then to love one another. Whatever this may mean in terms of our personal circumstances, teach us, Father, to love one another. We pray in Christ's name, Amen.